FOREWORD BY PAUL

EXPOSING THE ENEMY

DARRYL S. BRISTER

Published By:
Jasher Press & Co.
www.jasherpress.com
customerservice@jasherpress.com
1.888.220.2068
New Bern, NC 28561

Copyright© 2014

ISBN: 978-0692021972

First Edition
Printed and bound in the United States of America

FOREWORD BY PAUL S. MORTON SR.

EXPOSING THE ENEMY

DARRYL S. BRISTER

JASHER PRESS & CO.

DEDICATION

To my Father and mentor who is now in heaven, the late Ellie D. Brister, Sr. A man among men. To Rev. John C. Raphael, Jr. who slipped away from me less than a year ago, thanks for the golden moments and nuggets.

To every member of the Body of Christ seeking and sensing a higher call of God upon their lives; particularly those who feel they are unworthy to be used by God in a supernatural way because of failures, struggles, mishaps, and personal inconsistencies.

To my children; they are all unique and special in their own ways: (my firstborn) DARRLYNN and her fiancé CLIFTON ,(my name-sake) DARRYL Jr., (my testimony) DARIEL and her husband SHANE, (my promise) TREY and last but certainly not least (my poodie n princess) TYZA.

ACKNOWLEDGEMENTS

I am so thankful for the wonderful people the Lord has placed in my life to be a blessing to me as I continue in the perpetual ministry of God.

To my beautiful wife and best friend, Dionne Devell, who shares me with thousands. For more than two decades now, you've been the same consistent, compassionate, and considerate wife, friend, mother, and First Lady! Wow!

To my praying and loving Mother, Earlie Mae Brister, to my siblings: Elder SANDRA DORSEY who's my personal intercessor. All of my life you've prayed for me and I'm thankful and grateful. Your strength is inspiring. DOROTHY, my only big brother E.DAVID (Kippie) (DEMETRA), DIANE (DENNIS), JULIA (BRYANT), GWEN (AL), y'all just simply light up my life!

Presiding Bishop Paul S. Morton, Sr., Pastor Debra B. Morton, Bishop Nathaniel Holcomb, Presiding Bishop - Elect Joseph Warren Walker, Tiers of Leadership of the Full Gospel Baptist Church Fellowship, and staff of DSB Ministries – thanks for your inspiration.

To my executive Pastor and son Elder Jeremy (Catrice) Brister, I can't express in words how grateful and thankful I am of your maturation process. To my spiritual sons, I'm so proud of your all! Bishop A. G.Mullen, Bishop Herbert Andrew, Bishop Joseph Carter, General Overseer Dennis R. Hebert, Jr, Pastors Eric A. Williams, E. Chris Washington, Serge Francios , Danny Donaldson , and all of the beautiful and supportive members of the Beacon Light Baptist Church Family, Abundant Life, Rose Hill, and

Covenant Partners of DSB ministries, To the Pastors who are connected and submitted to me through DSBIA, I love all of you

CONTENTS

FOREWORD

From a spiritual father to a spiritual son... I know him to be a great son who is very easy to mentor. Because of his great ability, Bishop Darryl S. Brister is one of God's most anointed preachers and a notable pastor. He pastors one of the fastest growing churches in America, and now, he comes forward and captivates our minds in this powerful book, *Exposing the Enemy*.

Satan – the enemy – has been undiscovered for too long. People, things and even God have been taking the blame and the devil gets away without a challenge, and we end up being mad with everyone except the enemy.

In this remarkable book, Bishop Darryl Brister said, "Enough is enough!" He shows us how to recognize the enemy and exposes the father of deceit. He deals with the source of the problem, but he is obligated to give us the solution. *Exposing the Enemy* shows us how to prepare ourselves to win the war against the enemy. We can overcome the enemy by the blood of the Lamb and by the word of our testimony.

11

Bishop Brister shares with us some of the things he had to wrestle in his own life, and how he gained the victory by **"Exposing the Enemy."** He doesn't pull any punches – he tells it like it is!

–By Bishop Paul S. Morton, Sr.

International Presiding Bishop
Full Gospel Baptist Church Fellowship

INTRODUCTION

So then faith cometh by hearing, and hearing by the word of God.

Romans 10:17

In this book we will be examining a subject of vital importance to every believer: spiritual warfare. I believe the information you will receive from this study is life-changing. The principles you will learn in this series of lessons can ultimately transform your entire life, if you so desire.

According to Romans 10:17 faith comes by hearing, and hearing by the Word of God. It is my prayer that as you read these pages and allow the Holy Spirit to speak to you through them you will be blessed. I pray you will be enlightened and empowered to recognize and overcome all the cunning wiles of the enemy and to reap all the bountiful benefits that are rightfully yours as a blood-bought child of God.

CHAPTER 1

KNOWING YOUR ENEMY

My people are destroyed for lack of knowledge: because thou hast rejected knowledge, I will also reject thee, that thou shalt be no priest to me: seeing thou hast forgotten the law of thy God, I will also forget thy children.**

Hosea 4:6

We always quote that Scripture, **My people are destroyed for lack of knowledge...** But it doesn't stop there. In it God goes on to say ... **because thou hast rejected knowledge, I will also reject thee, that thou shalt be no priest to me...**

We must realize that in this context God is dealing with the shepherds' ministry. The fact that God's people are being destroyed for a lack of knowledge is not their fault. It is the fault of the shepherds, because knowledge is not coming forth from the pulpit.

Today many preachers are being destroyed along with their people. The reason that is happening is that the preachers themselves are lacking in knowledge. That is what God means when He says... **seeing thou hast forgotten the law of thy God; I will also forget thy children**. How can anyone teach what he himself does not know?

We must realize that we are engaged in spiritual warfare. But spiritual warfare is not a subject that is taught in every church.

The reason so many people are being destroyed is that they are not being taught about the spiritual realm. Yet everything we deal with in this life has a spiritual origin. If we have no knowledge of spiritual things, we will be destroyed.

That is why I have written this book, to help believers learn to recognize our spiritual enemy and know how to deal with him in the spiritual realm.

SPIRITUAL KNOWLEDGE

This I say therefore, and testify in the Lord, that ye henceforth walk not as other Gentiles walk, in the vanity of their mind,

16

Having the understanding darkened, being alienated from the life of God through the ignorance that is in them, because of the blindness of their heart.

Ephesians 4: 17, 18

There are a lot of Christians today who are being destroyed because they are alienated or separated from the life of God. They do not have a personal, one-on-one, everyday working relationship with the Lord.

Part of the reason is that their understanding is darkened because they have never been taught about spiritual things. Many ministers preach so far over the heads of the congregation, their people cannot understand what they are saying.

The Word of God was never meant to be complicated. It is supposed to be within the grasp of everyone's understanding. But today many people are alienated from the life of God's because of the blindness of their hearts and their ignorance of His Word.

Many try to read the Bible for themselves, but claim they cannot understand it. The reason they cannot understand it is that it is a spiritual book. In 1 Corinthians 2:14, we read... **the natural man receiveth not the things of the Spirit of God: for they are foolishness unto him: neither can he know them, because they are spiritually discerned.** That's why the Bible says, **Trust in the Lord**

with all thine heart; and lean not unto thine own understanding (Prov. 3:5)

The reason we must trust God and not our own understanding is that our human minds cannot comprehend the things of God, the things of the spiritual realm – things like spiritual warfare.

SPIRITUAL WARFARE

(For though we walk in the flesh, we do not war after the flesh:

For the weapons of our warfare are not carnal, but mighty through God to the pulling down of strong holds).

2 Corinthians 10:3, 4

Warfare is defined as a struggle between competing entities. In other words, warfare is conflict. Wherever we are at the moment, whatever we may be doing, whether we realize it or not, we are in the midst of conflict. We are warring with many things – in our minds, our marriages, our homes, our jobs. None of us will ever be able to escape conflict, because it is spiritual, not physical. Demons are real and they are at war against us.

Many people think demons are something that existed only in Bible days. Often the reason we do not recognize demons today is that they sometimes take on

18

different forms from Bible times. Crack cocaine, for example, is caused by demonic influence. Crime against our brothers is caused by demonic influence. Rebellion against parents is demonically inspired.

People are being destroyed today because of ignorance. God is making His knowledge available to them, but they are refusing it. They are trying to wage warfare in the flesh rather than in the Spirit.

Other people are not our problem. Our spouses, our parents, or children, our bosses, or our neighbors are not the problem. In the warfare in which you and I are engaged, a .38 special, a nine-millimeter pistol, or even an Uzzi machine gun won't do us any good, because our enemy is not physical, but spiritual. As Paul tells us in this passage, in order to wage spiritual warfare, we must rely on spiritual weapons, because we have a spiritual enemy.

KNOW YOUR ENEMY

For we wrestle not against flesh and blood, but against principalities, against powers, against the rulers of the darkness of this world, against spiritual wickedness in high places.

Ephesians 6:12

Paul tells us that we wrestle not against flesh and blood, but against powerful spiritual enemies.

As believers, we must not become confused about who our enemy is and begin to wage war against one another. If we do, we will be destroyed.

We must use our spiritual weapons against our spiritual enemy in order to pull down the strongholds he is trying to build up in our minds and hearts. But before we can wage war against him and destroy his strongholds, we must know who he is, and often that takes discipline and training.

I had the wonderful, blessed privilege of spending a very important period of my life in the military. I didn't know why God led me join the United States Army, but I am glad He did. I can see now that He had to take me away from my family and friends to bring me to a place where I knew no one and was totally dependent upon Him.

God used the military as a vehicle to get my undivided attention. When I first arrived on base, I thought, "Lord, how in the world did I get myself into this?" The strange part is that I wasn't even drafted, I joined voluntarily!

I soon learned that everything I had heard about the military was true. I was put through rigorous physical and psychological training. My body and mind had never been so inflicted with pain and trauma.

The first thing the army did was shave my head. When I was sent in for a haircut, I sat down in the chair and told the barber, "Take a little bit off the sides." He took everything off! He didn't even leave me a line or a part – nothing!

Now I am able to look back on experiences like that and see a spiritual application. I can see that when we become part of God's army, He takes us and subjects us to all kinds of distasteful things in order to train us for warfare. One of the first things He does is teach us to get our minds off ourselves and onto Jesus Christ. By developing a relationship with Him, we will be much more sensitive to the enemy and his maneuvers.

As members of the army of the Lord, our problem is that too often we like getting all dressed up in our uniforms, but we don't want to fight. Before we can fight effectively, we must be trained.

My training as a soldier begun at 4:30 every morning when we were roused from our bunks and sent out to run up mountains – not hills, but mountains. We would run so long and hard our legs would give out on us, and we would fall down. Three times a day we would run for three miles at a time – for a total of nine miles a day.

At the time I couldn't understand what all that harsh treatment was all about. Now I see what the drill instructors were trying to do. They were trying to get us into shape physically, because a soldier cannot afford to get short winded after running a block.

That's what God is doing to His people today. He is training us for warfare, and that warfare has already begun. It is going on all around us day and night. If we are to survive and be victorious, we must get into shape and learn to fight effectively.

At the same time the army was working on altering our outward appearance and conditioning our physical bodies, it was also working on developing our inner resources. For example, we would be suddenly awakened in the middle of the night and commanded to fall into formation. As soon as we had done that, we would be ordered to go back to our bunks and fall asleep. What was the purpose of that kind of frustrating exercise? It was to train us to endure psychological and emotional stress, as well as physical hardship.

Another part of our mental training was instant identification. We would be shown a set of contrasting cards with pictures of American and Soviet arms and equipment and told to memorize them. At any moment our instructors would flash a card with a picture of a gas mask or a rifle or a tank, and demand that we correctly identify whether it was American or Soviet. If we guessed wrong, we would be subjected to some kind of punishment.

That principle holds true for us as Christians. Often there is a fine line between a devil and a believer. The devil is not running around in a red suit with a forked tail, pointed horns, and a pitchfork. The devil can be tall, dark, and handsome. The devil can be a perfect 36-24-36.

We must be on our guard, because if our enemy came at us looking like the devil, we would recognize him right away. Regardless of his appearance, we must be able to recognize our enemy and distinguish him so we can oppose him and defeat him.

The last unit I belonged to was Bravo Company of the 532nd MI Battalion. The letters MI stood for Military Intelligence. As an intelligence unit, our battalion motto was "Know Your Enemy." Later on, that slogan became spiritual revelation to me.

To recognize and expose our spiritual enemy, we must know something about the spiritual realm. To do that, we must go back before the existence of this physical realm to consider the pre-Adamite world.

Pre-Adamite World

In the beginning God created the heaven and the earth.

And the Lord God formed man of the dust of the ground, and breathed into his nostrils the breath of life; and man became a living soul.

And the Lord God planted a garden eastward in Eden; and there he put the man whom he had formed.

Genesis 1:1, 2:7, 8

We know from the first chapters of the book of Genesis that God created the heavens and the earth. We also know that God created a man by the name of Adam and a woman by the name of Eve and placed them in a garden called the Garden of Eden.

But the Garden of Eden was not the beginning. Even Genesis was not the beginning. There was something called the pre-Adamite world, a spiritual realm which existed before creation.

When the Bible says, "In the beginning," it is not referring to the beginning of everything that now exists, but only to the beginning of the physical realm in which you and I live today. Before that realm came into existence, there was a spiritual realm inhabited by spiritual beings: God and His angels.

In this spiritual realm, Almighty God sat on His throne and reigned over His angels. Among those angels there were archangels: 1) Gabriel, the messenger, whose job was to take the word of God and present it to the other angelic beings, 2) Michael, the warrior, whose job was to wage war on behalf of God, and 3) Lucifer, the worship angel, whose job was to lead praise and worship in heaven.

PRAISE and WORSHIP

But the hour cometh, and now is, when the true worshippers shall worship the Father in spirit and in truth: for the Father seeketh such to worship him.

God is a Spirit: and they that worship him must worship him in spirit and in truth.

John 4:23, 24

Why is worship so important to us today? It is important because, as we will see, Lucifer, filled with pride, rebelled against God and was cast out of heaven – leaving no one to lead worship. That's what Jesus meant when He said that the Father is looking for those who will worship Him in spirit and in truth.

In my years of ministry, I have discovered there are a lot of people who go to church, but who know nothing about praise and worship. There is a difference between praise and worship. Unless we understand that difference, we will never be able to truly worship the Father in a way that is pleasing to Him.

We praise God for *what He has done*. That's why we praise Him regardless of what is going on in our lives, knowing that He is worthy of all praise. We may not have an overflowing bank account, but if we have shoes on our

25

feet, clothes on our back, and a roof over our head, that is enough reason to praise God from Whom all blessings flow.

But while we praise God for what He has done, we worship Him for *Who He is*. We worship Him as the Way-Maker, the Provider, our Shield and Defender, our Buckler and Strong Tower, the Balm of Gilead, the Lily of the Valley, the Rose of Sharon, and on and on.

That is what Lucifer was supposed to do, but he failed and fell.

WHO IS LUCIFER?

Moreover the word of the Lord came unto me, saying, Son of man, take up a lamentation upon the king of Tyrus, and say unto him, Thus saith the Lord God; Thou sealest up the sum, full of wisdom, and perfect in beauty.

Thou hast been in Eden the garden of God; every precious stone was thy covering, the sardius, topaz, and the diamond, the beryl, the onyx, and the jasper, the sapphire, the emerald, and the carbuncle, and gold: the workmanship of the tabrets and of thy pipes was prepared in thee in the day that thou wast created.

Thou art the anointed cherub that covereth; and I have set thee so thou wast upon the holy mountain of God; thou hast walked up and down in the midst of the

26

stones of fire. Thou wast perfect in thy ways from the day that thou was created, till iniquity was found in thee.

Ezekiel 28:11-15

This passage of prophetic Scripture relates to the time before creation and refers not to a natural or physical king, but to a spiritual ruler.

The earthly king of Tyrus at this time was Ithobalus II, but this could not be the person described here. In this passage the Lord tells His prophet to take up a lamentation against this ruler who is full of wisdom and perfect in beauty, which is a precise description of Lucifer before his fall.

Adam is the only human being who was not born; like the angels, he was created by God. The angels do not have mothers and fathers, because they are created beings. Therefore the person to whom this word from the Lord is directed could not have been a human king, because no human being was ever created by God to live in the heavenly realm, as this ruler was. Nor, is there any human being other than Jesus who has ever been perfect in all his ways.

In heaven, Lucifer was a guardian cherub, a beautiful, perfect angel covered in precious jewels. In fact, the name Lucifer means "the morning star"[1] or "son of the morning" (Isaiah 14:12). But it is not proper to refer to him by that name anymore, because he is no longer a beautiful, perfect angel. Now he is a fallen, rebellious angel named Satan.

LUCIFER'S PRIDE AND FALL

How art thou fallen from heaven, O Lucifer, son of the morning! How art thou cut down to the ground, which didst weaken the nations!

For thou hast said in thine heart, I will ascend into heaven, I will exalt my throne above the stars of God: I will sit also upon the mount of the congregation, in the sides of the north:

I will ascend above the heights of the clouds; I will be like the most High.

Yet thou shalt be brought down to hell, to the sides of a pit.

Isaiah 14:12-15

---

[1] James Strong, "Hebrew and Chaldee Dictionary," in Strong's Exhaustive Concordance of the Bible (Nashville: Abingdon, 1890), p. 32, entry #1966, s.v. "Lucifer," Isaiah 14:12.

Lucifer's role as an archangel was that of worship leader. He was in charge of praise and worship to God. But he became filled with pride and began to boast of what all he would do: "I will, I will, I will."

Pride is not of God. It is an evil spirit – an imp or demon – and it will lead to a downfall, just as it did for Lucifer.

Lucifer Is Cast Down to Earth

And there was war in heaven: Michael and his angels fought against the dragon; and the dragon fought and angels,

And prevailed not; neither was their place found anymore in heaven.

And the great dragon was cast out, that old serpent, called the Devil, and Satan, which deceiveth the whole world: he was cast out into the earth, and his angels were cast out with him.

And I heard a loud voice saying in heaven, Now is come salvation, and strength, and the kingdom of our God, and the power of his Christ: for the accuser of our brethren is cast down, which accused them before our God day and night.

Revelation 12:7-10

Lucifer was so filled with pride he tried to make himself greater than God. He formed a rebellion in heaven and led one-third of the angels in battle against the army of the Lord under Michael, the warrior angel. But he was defeated.

The Lord said to Lucifer, "Because of your attitude of pride and rebellion, you cannot stay in heaven; therefore, I will banish you forever."

Lucifer, the anointed cherub, was not satisfied to be second in command, so he tried to overthrow God's Kingdom. But he ended up being expelled from it and cast down to the earth where he became known as Satan, the deceiver and accuser.

THE DEVIL IS LOOSE...

Therefore rejoice, ye heavens, and ye that dwell in them. Woe to the inhabiters of the earth and of the sea! For the devil is come down unto you, having great wrath, because he knowth that he hath but a short time.

Revelation 12:12

So Lucifer, now known as Satan, was cast down to earth. By the time Adam and Eve came on the scene, the devil and his demons were already here. In his wrath Satan began to try to get back at God by deceiving the man and woman the Lord had created and put in authority over the earth. He has never stopped doing that.

We must realize that Satan's number one job is to get people to disobey God. Why? Because he hates God and is in rebellion against Him. That is the spiritual battle between Satan and God that you and I find ourselves in the midst of today.

The devil tries to get at God by using us. Every time he succeeds in deceiving us into disobeying God, he has won a victory. That's why our desire and our prayer should be that in everything we are always totally obedient to the Lord. More than anything else in this life, we should want to do what is pleasing in God's sight. If we are tempted to do anything that is not pleasing to God or that is not in accordance with His will, we can be sure where that temptation is coming from – our enemy, the devil.

...BUT VICTORY IS OURS!

... in all things we are more than conquerors through him that loved us.

Romans 8:37

Too often we find ourselves fighting the wrong person. We must understand that our enemy is not other people; it is the devil and his demons. We will never experience any peace or victory in our lives as long as we are fussing and fighting with one another.

31

As the children of God, we are destined to win. We have no real problems, because the outcome has already been decided. The ultimate victory in this life is ours. Why then should we go through life angry and upset? Why should we worry and fret? Why should we lose sleep or our appetite? It's not worth it.

As God's beloved children, we should know that our lives are in His hands. We should also know that we have an enemy who hates us because he hates our heavenly Father. As marked men and woman, we should expect the devil to try to cause problems for us.

One time a certain person came to me to give me a word of warning, saying, "Pastor, the Lord showed me the devil is after you." I thought to myself, "As if I didn't know that already!"

Another time I received an anonymous letter addressed simply to the pastor of Beacon Light Baptist Church. The envelope was marked "Personal and Private." There was no return address, and the letter began, "From a servant of God."

Basically, what the writer of that letter was telling me was that what I was preaching about spiritual warfare was wrong, and I should stop preaching it. Instead of causing me to quit, that letter just motivated me to preach even harder. I knew it was a device of the devil who was trying to discourage me from delivering the message God had placed on my heart.

We saw that faith comes by hearing, and hearing by the Word of God. We have read that God's people are destroyed for lack of knowledge. That is why I must keep on preaching this message even when there is opposition to it. I know that every time we hear the Word of God, our faith is strengthened, and we are encouraged, and empowered to resist the devil and his demons that are out to deceive and destroy.

CHAPTER 2

YOUR OWN WORST ENEMY

B *ut the children of Israel committed a trespass*
regarding the accursed things, for Achan the son of
Carmi, the son of Zabdi, the son of Zerah, of the
tribe of Judah, took of the accursed things; so the anger of
the Lord burned against the children of Israel. And Joshua
sent men from Jericho to Ai, which is beside Beth-aven, on
the east side of Beth-el, and spoke to them, saying, "Go up
and spy out the country." And the men went up and viewed
Ai. And they returned to Joshua and said to him, "Let not
all the people go up, but let about two or three thousand
men go up and smite Ai; and make not all the people to
labour thither; for they are but few." So there went up
thither of the people about three thousand men: and they
fled before the men Ai. And the men of Ai smote of them
about thirty and six men: for they chased them from before
the gate even unto Shebarim, and smote them in the going
down: wherefore the hearts of the people melted, and
became as water. And Joshua rent his clothes, and fell to
the earth upon his face before the ark of the Lord until

35

eventide, he and the elders of Israel, and they put dust upon their heads. And Joshua said, "Alas, O Lord God, wherefore hast thou at all brought this people over Jordan, to deliver us into the hand of the Amorites, to destroy us? Would to God we had been content, and dwelt on the other side Jordan! O Lord, what shall I say, when Israel turneth their backs before their enemies! For the Canaanites and the inhabitants of the land shall hear of it, and shall environ us round, and cut off our name from the earth: and what wilt thou do unto thy great name? And the Lord said unto Joshua, Get thee up; wherefore liest thou thus upon thy face? Israel hath sinned, and they have also transgressed my covenant which I commanded them: for they have even taken of the accursed thing, and have also stolen, and dissembled also, and they have put it even among their own stuff. -Joshua 7:1-11

Once upon a time a rat looked through a crack in the wall to see the farmer and his wife opening a package. What food might it contain? He was aghast to discover that it was a rat trap. Retreating to the farmyard the rat proclaimed the warning; "There is a rat trap in the house, a rat trap in the house!"

The chicken clucked and scratched, raised her head and said, "Excuse me, Mr. Rat, I can tell this is a grave concern to you, but it is of no consequence to me. I cannot be bothered by it."

The rat turned to the pig and told him, "There is a rat trap in the house, a rat trap in the house!"

36

"I am so very sorry Mr. Rat," sympathized the pig, "but there is nothing I can do about it, but pray. Be assured that you are in my prayers."

The rat turned to the cow. She said, "Like wow, Mr. Rat. A rat trap. I am in no grave danger. Duh?"

So the rat returned to the house, head down and dejected, to face the farmer's rat trap alone. That very night a sound was heard throughout the house, like the sound of a rat trap catching its prey. The farmer's wife rushed to see what was caught. In the darkness, she did not see that it was a venomous snake whose tail the trap had caught. The snake bit the farmer's wife. The farmer rushed her to the hospital.

She returned home with a fever. Now everyone knows that you treat a fever with fresh chicken soup, so the farmer took his hatchet to the farmyard for the soup's main ingredient.

His wife's sickness continued so that friends and neighbors came to sit with her around the clock. To feed them the farmer butchered the pig.

The farmer's wife did not get well. She died and so many people came for her funeral that the farmer had the cow slaughtered to provide meat for all of them to eat.

So the next time you hear that someone is facing a problem and think that it does not concern you, remember that when there is a rat trap in the house, the whole farmyard is at risk.

This truth could not be more relevant than what we see in Joshua 7:1-11. One household in Israel caused an entire battle to be lost - the Battle of Ai.

We could argue that just because some families are in trouble in our world today, it does not mean we should be alarmed. That statement could be nothing further than the truth. The disintegration of even one household affects us all!

The battle of Ai was supposed to be a pushover in comparison to the great battle that had just been won at Jericho. But now General Joshua is perplexed to determine what went wrong in a battle that should have gone into the history book as an overwhelming victory.

God revealed the problem to be a "household" problem. In fact, many of the problems facing our world and the church today are "household" problems.

The word "household" appears 61 times in the authorized version of the Bible. It's a great biblical word because it covers everyone living in a particular house, not just the nuclear family.

The word "households" covers not only two-parent families, but also single-parent families, blended families, multi-generational families, and etc. Consequently, what the Bible teaches us about "households" applies to every one of us.

Let's consider the household of Achan and discover "How to Be Your Own Worst Enemy At Home." The insights that are revealed in the scriptures are truly amazing.

First of all, **you will become your own worst enemy at home if you neglect your spiritual responsibilities.** The issue with Achan's sin centers around "the accursed things." Joshua 7:1 - *"But the children of Israel committed a trespass regarding the accursed things, for Achan...took of the accursed things; so the anger of the LORD burned against the children of Israel."*

What made the things that Achan took "accursed?" When Joshua informed his military staff about the impending victory at Jericho he gave these instructions in Joshua 6:17-19: *"Now the city shall be doomed by the LORD to destruction, it and all who are in it. Only Rahab the harlot shall live, she and all who are in her house, because she hid the messengers that we sent. And you, by all means keep yourselves from the accursed things, lest you become accursed when you take of the accursed things, and make the camp of Israel a curse, and trouble it. But all the gold, and vessels of bronze and iron, are consecrated to*

39

the LORD; they shall come into the treasury of the LORD."
Some things belong to the LORD.

Not only should we honor God with a certain portion of our material things. Certainly the things that Aachan took were material things. But think about it... We should also honor God with our time. Sadly we spend more time with the remote control and the telephone in our hands at home than we do the Bible or good Christian reading material. Like the wife who was coming down the stairs and asked her husband laying on the sofa what he had been doing.

He replied, "Killing flies."

She said, "How many have you killed so far?"

He said, "Five, three males and two females."

She said, "How did you figure that out?"

He replied, "Three were sitting on the remote and two were sitting on the phone."

Seriously, stop and consider how much time you spend at home giving attention to spiritual things. I'm not suggesting you walk around like a Pharisee with a verse of scripture taped to your head, or that you throw your television set out the window. But do we really see what Achan's problem was? He wasn't willing to give to God what belonged to Him.

40

And whenever we take the accursed thing; it curses us and our household! We cannot live spiritually successful family lives without God! That's the foundation. By the way, do you remember that Rahab, who had previously lived an immoral life, saved her family by her dedication to spiritual things?

Secondly, **You become your own worst enemy at home when you have sinful secrets.** Achan knew what he did was wrong and he had to hide the evidence under the floor of his tent. Joshua 7:21 - *"When I saw among the spoils a beautiful Babylonian garment, two hundred shekels of silver, and a wedge of gold weighing fifty shekels, I coveted them and took them. And there they are, hidden in the earth in the midst of my tent, with the silver under it."* Discovery time always appears.

We try to hide things from God and others and sooner or later they come to the surface. The Bible puts it this way: *"Be sure your sin will find you out."* (Numbers 32:23c) God doesn't have to come with a search warrant. Sin has its own natural consequences and they just start cropping up.

Oh the blessings of obedience! And oh, the curse of disobedience! Let the Holy Spirit talk to you. What do you think you are hiding from God in your home? Do you think it's securely hidden in your computer? No, think again. Do you think it's safely under lock and key in some cabinet? Do you believe that your thoughts of jealousy, bitterness, hatred, etc. are not known to God? Many times they are also realized by others because our thoughts are often betrayed by our actions.

God's warnings here in the story of Achan are for our advantage. Destroy the accursed things today. Ask God to help you and He will.

Jesus said, *"And if your right eye causes you to sin, pluck it out and cast it from you; for it is more profitable for you that one of your members perish, than for your whole body to be cast into hell. And if your right hand causes you to sin, cut it off and cast it from you; for it is more profitable for you that one of your members perish, than for your whole body to be cast into hell."* (Matthew 5:29, 30)

Now Jesus was using a hyperbole. He wasn't literally telling us to mutilate our bodies. Rather, He was telling us to deal immediately and drastically with those things that harm our spiritual life.

Achan's hidden sin affected his entire household. Do yourself and your family a favor and get rid of the accursed thing. It will drastically improve things at your household!

Thirdly, **we become our own worst enemy at home when we fail to give glory to God.** Joshua 7:19 - *"So Joshua said to Achan, "My son, I beg you, give glory to* *the LORD God of Israel, and make confession to Him, and tell me now what you have done; do not hide it from me."*

What do you do to honor God in your household? Those of us who worship the only true God might consider being ashamed of ourselves. No, I'm honestly not trying to play the Holy Spirit.

But come on! We have our big screen television set (and no I'm not suggesting they're sinful), our mega-powerful stereo systems, our state of the art computers, our cell phones, and all the other gadgets of twenty-first century opulence - but what do we have that honors God in our home?

Here are some suggestions of things that honor God.

1. A Bible for every person in your household. Children's Bibles in picture form for the very young; youth study Bibles for the teens; Bible study helps for the adults. And by the way, read the Bible; don't just use it for decoration!

2. Good Christian magazines. You don't even have to subscribe - learn to trade with other Christ-followers or shop for good deals at thrift stores or yard sales.

3. Good Christian books, fiction and non-fiction.

4. Good Christian music.

5. Good Christian art.

43

6. A place to entertain other Christ-followers or others who we pray will become followers of Christ.

7. Verses of scripture and missionary prayer cards on the refrigerator, the mirrors in our bathrooms, and etc.

Did you know that last year Americans gave: $2.9 billion dollars to overseas missions? But they also gave $7.7 billion to see movies, $13 billion to buy chocolate, $23 billion to buy toys, $23 billion to buy stuff for their pets, $24 billion for jewelry, $58 billion for soft drinks, $85 billion for lawn and garden care, and $354 billion to eat out at restaurants!

Perhaps if Achan had thought about putting things that honored God in his tent he wouldn't have been tempted to covet the accursed things.

If you honor God in your home you will not need glittering substitutes and you will not become your own worst enemy. When Achan's sin was dealt with the people of God won the battle at the city of Ai. (Joshua 8) Deal with the enemy in your household, even if its yourself, and you will begin to see great victories!

CHAPTER 3

IGNORANCE IS A KILLER

The Spirit of the Lord God is upon me; because the Lord hath anointed me to preach good tidings unto the meek; he hath sent me to bind up the brokenhearted, to proclaim liberty to the captives, and the opening of the prison to them that are bound;

To proclaim the acceptable year of the Lord, and the day of vengeance of our God; to comfort all that mourn;

To appoint unto them that mourn in Zion, to give unto them beauty for ashes, the oil of joy for mourning, the garment of praise for the spirit of heaviness...

Isaiah 61:1-3

In the next three chapters we are going to be examining the subject of the proper dress for battle. If we are to be successful in waging spiritual warfare, there are certain things we need to put on, just as there are certain things we need to take up.

As we have seen from 2 Corinthians 10: 3, 4, although we walk in the flesh, we do not wage war in the flesh. Instead, we use powerful spiritual weapons to pull down the strongholds of our spiritual enemy Lucifer, son of the morning, who was cast out of heaven down to earth where he has now become Satan, the accuser of the brethren. Since the devil is constantly scheming and planning to destroy us, for our own protection we must learn to dress properly.

As the Body of Christ, we are not supposed to be a defeated Church, but a victorious Church. To do that, we must be on our guard at all times **lest Satan should get an advantage of us: for we are not ignorant of his devices** (2 Corinthians 2:11). As we have seen, God has warned us that ignorance, or a lack of knowledge, will lead to our destruction. That is also true of fear.

For too long the Church of Jesus Christ has been running from the enemy like a dog with its tail tucked between its legs, I believe God is now raising up all who will take a stand against the devil and let him know he cannot have our homes, our children, our families, our society.

Since weapons of the flesh are ineffective in spiritual warfare, we must have spiritual weapons. For protection against our spiritual enemy, we must also be clothed in spiritual garments. In the passage from the prophet Isaiah, the Bible talks about the garment of praise for a spirit of heaviness.

Have you ever awakened in a bad mood? Have you ever gone through an entire day feeling sluggish, depressed, and oppressed? That is an example of the spiritual warfare. That day the devil sent a particular demon to attack you with a spirit of heaviness.

The next time that happens, you need to recognize it for what it is – a spiritual attack. You need to put on the garment of praise to resist that spirit of heaviness. You need to begin to use the spiritual weapon of praise to overcome the devices of the enemy.

That's how you drive off evil spirits, by saying, "Lord, I am under attack, but in spite of how things may look or how I feel at the moment, I know that You are still worthy of praise."

Besides the spirit of heaviness, Satan has many other devices of spiritual warfare. Sickness is caused by a spirit. Drug additions are caused by demonic spirit. Crime is caused by demonic influence.

No matter how many jails and prisons we may build, we will never solve the crime problem, because once they are full, we will just have to release criminals who will go right back out and commit more crimes. It doesn't matter who we elect to public office, how many police officers we employ, or how many new or more powerful guns we purchase, we will still have crime to contend with until we learn we cannot wage spiritual warfare with physical weapons.

FREEDOM FROM SPIRITUAL STRONGHOLDS

If the Son therefore shall make you free, ye shall be free indeed.

John 8:36

Part of the problem with our society today is that too many of us in the Church still have strongholds in our own lives. As Christians we should not be bound by anything. Whatever holds us in bondage is a stronghold.

In John 8:36 Jesus told us that anyone who has been set free by Him is free indeed. There are many of us who love the Lord with all our heart and mind and soul, but we still have weakness in our life. We all have things we simply cannot seem to stop doing, although we may have tried to stop for years. The reason we can't stop doing those things is that they have become strongholds – spiritual strongholds – and the only way they can be pulled down is by spiritual power.

The devil is a powerful enemy, but for years we have given him too much credit. Yes, he is a power to be reckoned with, but we must remember that greater is He Who is in us than he who is in the world. (1 John 4:4) Yes, Satan does have power, but we must remember what the Lord told us in Luke 10:19: Behold, **I give unto you power to tread on serpents and scorpions, and over all the power of the enemy: and nothing shall by any means hurt you.**

The reason so many Christians are being defeated is that they do not realize the power and authority that are theirs as the children of God. That's what Paul was referring to when he wrote to the church in Corinth explaining to them that the weapons of our warfare are not carnal but mighty through God to the pulling down of spiritual strongholds.

If you and I will learn to dress for spiritual battle and use the spiritual weapons God has provided for us, we will be able to walk in victory every day of our life. Although we walk in the flesh, we do not war in the flesh. Therefore, we do not clothe ourselves in the flesh, but in the Spirit of God. Just as we get dressed physically every day, so we must get dressed spiritual every day.

49

THE POWER OF GOD'S SPIRIT

Finally, my brethren, be strong in the Lord, and in the power of his might.

Ephesians 6:10

In Ephesians 6:10-18 Paul began to conclude his message to the church in Ephesus by telling them to be strong in the Lord and in the power of His might.

Now we are undressed. We are standing with the filthy rags of our own unrighteousness to cover us. The first mistake many us believers make is trying to be strong in the power of our own might. Too often we try to fight the devil by ourselves. On our own, you and I are no match for Satan. But Satan is no match for God. That's why we need to depend on the Lord and His mighty power.

But the person who is united to the Lord becomes one spirit with Him.

1 Corinthians 6:17 AMP

Every time you get dressed you should look in the mirror and say to yourself, "I am united with God today. I am one with Him. His power walks on this earth today wearing my flesh and my clothes. Together we form a mighty team. All the power and wisdom of God are in me today and I am dressed to kill every demon I meet."

The devil has been at this business of spiritual warfare for a long, long time. As we have seen, he was involved in it before the creation of the world, before man and woman ever came into being. That is one reason he was able to deceive them. Just as he succeeded with Adam and Eve in the Garden of Eden, so he is still succeeding with many people today- even with many of the children of God.

What is his goal? It is so simple. All Satan wants is for people to disobey God.

Why does Satan want us to disobey God? Because he knows that, like Adam and Eve in the Garden, when we have disobeyed God, we have broken fellowship with Him. Now we are undressed. We are standing with only the filthy rags of our own unrighteousness to cover us. We have lost contact with the power of God's might, and are left to try to withstand Satan on our own.

The devil knows that in our weakened condition he can destroy us at his will, as we read in 1 Peter 5:8: **Be sober, be vigilant; because your adversary the devil, as a roaring lion, walketh about, seeking whom he may devour.** That's why Paul wrote, urging us to be strong in the Lord, and in the power of His might.

THE ARMOR OF GOD

Put on the whole armor of God, that ye may be able to stand against the wiles of the devil.

Ephesians 6:11

Why does Paul tell us to put on the whole armor of God? So we can stand against the wiles of the devil. The word *wiles* can be understood as means, methods, or plans. It refers to the schemes, tactics, or strategies Satan uses to tempt us, deceive us, and lead us off into sin and disobedience to God, just as he did with Adam and Eve.

What we must realize is that the devil has a whole bag of tricks. If he can't get us one way, he will try something else. He knows our individual weaknesses, and he caters to them.

Some of us may have a weakness for food. If so, devil will play on that weakness by tempting us to overeat or eat the wrong kinds of food, things that are harmful to us and our health. He will see it that we are led places where we will be confronted with tempting foods, like company parties or backyard barbecues.

The devil plays for keeps – and he is an equal opportunity destroyer. It doesn't matter if we are young or old, male or female, short or tall, black or white, rich or poor, he wants us. That's why we must put on the whole armor of God in order to withstand his wiles, his schemes and strategies designed to lead us to our destruction.

Whether we want to or not, whether we like it or not, we must deal with Satan. Notice that I did not say we must make a deal with Satan. Peter has told us that our enemy the devil is out to devour us, and there is nothing any of us can do to make the devil lose his appetite.

Webster's dictionary defines devour as to eat up greedily or destroy, consume, and waste. The devil's business is stealing, killing, and destroying. Man was created from the dust of the earth. When man dies his body returns to dust.

It stands to reason then if we are dead, Satan has nothing tasty to bite into. When Carman wrote the song, *Satan Bite the Dust*, I believe the spiritual message was deep. If our flesh has died to sin, Satan cannot puncture dead flesh. If he tries, he'll have only a mouthful of dust.

Satan can only get a real bite of flesh that has not died – something in your old nature that has not yet been put on the altar and surrendered to God. He is always looking for anything alive to devour.

Satan is not going away, and he is not going to leave us alone. That's why it was so amusing when that person came to me with the revelation from the Lord that the devil was out to get me. I should have said, "Yes, I know, and he's out to get you too!" That's no deep revelation, it's just common sense.

Since the beginning of time Satan has sought to destroy righteous seed and history bears it out. Pharaoh ordered infants killed at the time of Moses' birth. Herod's order was the same at the time of Jesus' birth.

His tactics have not changed today. Well– meaning parents work hard to clothe their young men and women in designer jeans and the latest in tennis shoes, but often leave them uncovered spiritually.

Moses' mother hid him. Mary and Joseph left the country by divine order to protect their son. It is critical in this hour that we are covered spiritually and that we cover our children to protect them from Satan's destructive schemes.

If you and I are on God's side, the devil is after us. It's just that simple. That's why we must be properly dressed for battle. That's why we must put on the whole armor of God- because we are all wrestling with powerful spiritual enemies.

THE ENEMY IDENTIFIED

For we wrestle not against flesh and blood, but against principalities, against powers, against the rulers of the darkness of this world, against spiritual wickedness in high places.

Ephesians 6:12

You and I are flesh and blood, but we are not fighting against flesh and blood. Even though we may be killing one another in the streets of our cities, our problem is really not other people. As Paul is trying to tell us here, in this passage, our real enemies are not physical, but spiritual.

Every problem we have in this life originates from a spirit. Every circumstance has a spiritual foundation. If we cannot get along with our spouse or our brothers or sisters or our co-workers, that is a spiritual problem and requires a spiritual solution.

If we want to be victorious in life, we must learn to deal with the spiritual realm.

If we want to destroy a tree, we are wasting our time by cutting off the branches, because those branches will grow back. To destroy a tree, we must go underground and attack its roots. The same is true in our lives. To rid ourselves of our problems, we must get at their roots, which are spiritual, not material.

55

So who is our enemy? It is not other human beings, it is a spiritual being called Satan and his demons. Now we need to identify our Solution.

THE SOLUTION IDENTIFIED

When Jesus came into the coast of Caesarea Philippi, he asked his disciples, saying, Whom do men say that I the Son of man am?

And they said, Some say thou art John the Baptist some Elijah; and others, Jeremiah, or one of the prophets. He saith unto them, But whom say ye that I am? And Simon Peter answered and said, Thou art the Christ, the Son of the living God.

Matthew 16: 13-16

In the passage, Jesus is questioning His disciples to learn what people are saying about Him and how they identify Him. In 1990s paraphrase the conversation might go something like this:

Jesus: "Who am I?"

Disciples: "John the Baptist?"

Jesus: "No try again?"

Disciples: "Elijah?"

Jesus: "No, keep trying."

Disciples: "Jeremiah or one of the other prophets?"

Jesus: "No, try once more."

Peter: "I know. You're the Christ, the Son of the living God."

Jesus: "Right!"

Just as Peter and the disciples had to recognize Jesus for Who He was, so we must recognize Him for Who He is. And for that we need help.

Divine Revelation

And Jesus answered and said unto him, Blessed art thou, Simon Bar-jona: for flesh and blood hath not revealed it unto thee, but Father which is in heaven.

Matthew 16:17

Jesus told Peter he was blessed because his recognition of Who He was had not come from flesh and blood, but from a spiritual source – from God Himself. In other words, Peter did not have to go to school to learn to recognize spiritual truth, he received it by divine revelation.

The same is true for you and me today. We don't have to go to a Bible school or seminary to be able to recognize the source of our problems or the solution to those problems. We receive it the same way Peter did, by divine revelation.

As the children of God, spiritual knowledge and wisdom come to us not from flesh and blood, but directly from our Father in heaven.

Founded Upon the Rock

And I say also unto thee, That thou art Peter and upon this rock I will build my church; and the gates of hell shall not prevail against it.

Matthew 16:18

In Greek, the word translated *Peter* is *petros*, which means "(a piece of) rock."[2] What "rock" was Jesus referring to here? He was referring to the rock of divine revelation, not man's knowledge.

---

[2] James Strong, "Greek Dictionary of the New Testament," in *Strong's Exhaustive Concordance of the Bible* (Nashville: Abingdon, 1890), p.57, entry #4074, s.v. "Peter," Matthew 16:18

In John 12:32 Jesus said that if He was lifted up, He would draw all men unto Him. That means that the building up of the Church of Jesus Christ is not something done by man. That's why I will not allow Darryl Brister to be lifted up. I know it is not Darryl Brister who draws all men, it is Jesus. I don't want people to come hear me, I want them to come hear Jesus. He is the Rock the Church must be founded upon if it is to prevail against the gates of hell and bear much fruit for the Kingdom of God.

THE KEYS OF THE KINGDOM

And I will give unto thee the keys of the kingdom of heaven: and whatsoever thou shalt bind on earth shall be bound in heaven: and whatsoever thou shalt loose on earth shall be loosed in heaven.

Matthew 16: 19

When Jesus founded His Church on the rock of divine revelation, He gave it something special - the keys to the kingdom of heaven. That means if you and I have Jesus in our lives, we have the keys that give us the power to bind and loose on earth.

There are many Christians who love the Lord with all their heart and mind and soul, but who do not understand the authority that is theirs because of their relationship with the Lord. They do not appreciate the enormous power of prayer as a weapon of spiritual warfare.

When we set ourselves in prayer, Jesus has promised to stand behind us. When we bind the devil and his demons, Jesus agrees. When we loose healing, the Lord releases it also. We have the power to bind Satan from ourselves and others, and the power to loose him from ourselves and others. But to do that, we must learn to pray the prayer of faith.

THE PRAYER OF FAITH

Is any among you afflicted? let him pray. Is any merry? let him sing psalms. Is any sick among you? let him call for the elders of the church; and let them pray over him, anointing him with oil in the name of the Lord:

And the prayer of faith shall save the sick, and the Lord shall raise him up; and if he have committed sins, they shall be forgiven him. Confess your faults one to another, and pray for one another, that ye maybe healed. The effectual fervent prayer of a righteous man availeth much.

James 5:13-16

Prayer is warfare. Every time you and I begin to pray, a struggle breaks out. Often when we get on our knees, we don't know what to say. That happens because as soon as we try to turn our attention to spiritual matters, the devil attacks our mind. He sends a thousand thoughts to distract us from praying. Why? Because he knows the enormous power of prayer.

STAND FAST!

Therefore, brethren, stand fast, and hold the traditions which ye have been taught, whether by word, or our epistle.

2 Thessalonians 2:15

Many churches are founded upon tradition and that is not necessarily bad. Oftentimes tradition is good. I love traditions. But something is wrong when we allow the traditions of men to take precedence over the Word of God.

There are some church traditions that should be preserved. As a pastor, I don't believe in changing just to change. My philosophy is, if something is effective as it is, then it should be left alone.

Whatever we do, whether it is in agreement with our church traditions or not, we must hold on to the Word of God which tells us to stand fast against our spiritual enemy. And to do that, we must be properly dressed.

IGNORANCE IS A KILLER

CHAPTER 4

WARFARE IN THE HEAVENLIES

For we wrestle not against flesh and blood, but against principalities, against powers, against the rulers of darkness of this world, against spiritual wickedness in high places.

Ephesians 6:12

I believe God is raising up a people who are going to learn how to fight against the devil and his demons. For too long the devil has been destroying our homes, our families, our minds, and our bodies, and has been stagnating our spiritual growth. Now it is time for us to get fully and properly dressed for spiritual warfare.

As we have seen, Satan is a fallen angel named Lucifer who led one-third of the angels of heaven in a rebellion against God, but was cast out down to the earth where he still wages war against God by attacking His people and causing them to doubt and disobey Him. In order to resist the devil's wiles, we must receive spiritual revelation and learn to use the spiritual weapons that have been given to us by the Lord to defeat those demonic forces.

In Ephesians 6:12 we are told that we wrestle not against flesh and blood, but against different types of spiritual enemies. In 1 Corinthians 14, Paul tells us that everything in the Church should be done decently and in order because God is not the author of confusion, meaning that He is very organized. It may be surprising to some Christians to learn that Satan is also very organized. His army is very carefully structured.

In the United States Army, troops are divided into progressively larger groups, each led by an officer of higher rank. For example, there is a platoon of men which is led by a platoon commander, usually a lieutenant. Several platoons make up a company, which is led by a company commander, usually a captain. Several companies are grouped together to form a battalion, under the leadership of a battalion commander, usually a colonel. Several battalions form a brigade under the command of a brigadier general. Several brigades go together to make up a division, under the authority of a division commander, a higher-ranking general, and so on up the scale. The hierarchy of officers makes up what is called the chain of command which reaches all the way from the platoon level to the president of the United States who serves as commander-in-chief of all U.S. armed forces.

The same type of organizational structure and chain of command exists in Satan's army of demons. At the top, of course, is Satan himself, as commander-in-chief. Under him are what the Bible calls *principalities*. In Greek this word is *arche*, meaning a "chief."[3] So principalities may be thought of a chief rules, the highest-ranking demons in Satan's army.

Next highest in command are *powers*. In Greek this word is *exousia*, meaning "authority."[4] These receive their instructions from the principalities.

Next there are the *rulers of the darkness of this world*. In Greek the word is *kosmokrator*, meaning "a world ruler."[5]

Finally, there is the lowest-ranking demons referred to as *spiritual wickedness in high places*. These can be

---

[3] Strong, "Greek," p.16, entry #746, s.v. "principalities," Ephesians 6:12.

[4] Strong, "Greek," p.16, entry #746, s.v. "principalities," Ephesians 6:12.

[5] Strong, "Greek," p.43, entry #2888, s.v. "rulers," Ephesians 6:12.

thought of as the little demons with whom we come into contact on a daily basis in our homes or places of business, those like the demons of lust or lying. Although the *King James Version* says they inhabit "high places," other translations refer to their place of abode as "heavenly places," which can include the sanctuaries of our churches.

That means that even as we are gathered together to study the Word of God, there may be demonic forces in our midst. There may be among us spirits of envy, jealousy, strife, heaviness, depression, and so on.

Although we can't see them with our naked eyes, they are there, just as radio waves are there even though we are unable to perceive them with our unaided ears. If we bring a radio into church, we can pick up the radio signals that fill the room. In the same way, if we are spiritually attuned, we can distinguish the demonic forces that inhabit even our places of worship.

Since we are surrounded by such an army of demons, we need to be spiritually mature so we can discern them and know how to deal with them.

SPIRITUAL MATURITY

And he gave some, apostles; and some prophets; and some, evangelists; and some, pastors, and teachers;

For the perfecting of the saints, for the work of

the ministry, for the edifying of the body of Christ:

Till we all come in the unity of the faith, and of the knowledge of the Son of God, unto a perfect man, unto the measure of the stature of the fullness of Christ:

That we henceforth be no more children, tossed to and fro, and carried about with every wind of doctrine, by the sleight of men, and cunning craftiness, whereby they lie in wait to deceive;

But speaking the truth in love, may grow up into him in all things, which is the head, even Christ.

Ephesians 4:11-15

According to Paul, we in the Body of Christ have been given gifts - apostles, prophets, evangelists, pastors, and teachers - to help us grow to Christian maturity.

In 1 Corinthians 13:11 Paul wrote, **When I was a child, I spake as a child, I understood as a child, I thought as a child: but when I became a man, I put away childish things.** When we have truly matured spiritually, we will no longer speak, think, and act like children.

From example, we will stop trying to excuse our childish attitude and behavior by claiming we got up on the wrong side of the bed. The reason we are in bad mood is

68

not because of the bed itself, but because of the demons that surround it.

That's why when we get up in the morning, the first thing we should do is fall to our knees in prayer by the side of the bed,

The reason we wake up feeling bad is that we are under demonic attack. The best way to offset that attack is through prayer and praise. We might pray something like this: "Good morning, Lord. Thank You for watching over me last night and for allowing me to live to see another day. This is the day that You have made, Father, and I will rejoice and be glad in it" (Psalm 118:24).

That is one way of putting on the armor of God to withstand the wiles of the devil and his demonic army. That is one way of getting dressed for the day's battle, because often that battle will be waged in prayer, as we see in the life of Daniel.

DANIEL'S VISION

And in the four and twentieth day of the first month, as I was by the side of the great river, which is Hiddekel;

Then I lifted up mine eyes, and looked, and behold a certain man clothed in linen, whose loins were girded with fine gold of Uphaz:

His body also was liked the beryl, and his face as the appearance of lightning and his eyes as lamps of fire, and his arms and feet like in colour to polished brass, and the voice of his words like the voice of a multitude.

And I Daniel alone saw the vision: for the men that were with me saw not the vision; but a great quaking fell upon them, so that they fled to hide themselves.

Therefore, I was left alone, and saw this great vision, and there remained no strength in me: for my comeliness was turned in me into corruption and I retained no strength.

Yet heard I voice of his words: and when I heard the voice of his words, then was I in a deep sleep on my face, and my face toward the ground.

Daniel 10:4-9

Often when you and I pray for things it seems that our prayers are not being answered. There is a reason for that situation, as we will see in this incident in the life of Daniel. If we can grasp the reason for the delay in the manifestation of our prayers, it will literally change our whole outlook on prayer.

We must remember that since Satan knows how powerful prayer is, he will do everything he can to keep us from praying. Since he knows that when we pray, we bring God on the scene, the devil will keep us so busy we don't have time to pray. If he can't stop us from praying, he will do everything possible to interfere with our prayers.

If we start to pray and get so tired we fall asleep, that is a trick of the devil to interfere with our prayers. Satan causes us problems because he knows if we can establish and maintain a one-on-one, working relationship with God through daily prayer and fellowship, it is impossible for us to live a defeated life.

One time I was showing a longtime pastor friend of mine around our church building. He turned to me and said, "Pastor Brister, what are you doing? Whys is the Lord blessing you so much?"

"Brother, first of all, God is real to me," I said. "Second, I spend quality time with Him."

There's no big secret to success: you get out of anything what you put into it. The same is true spiritually as well as physically. If you want to be blessed, spend time with the Lord. Because you get out of God what you put into Him.

Some of us have a Sunday relationship with our heavenly Father. We don't speak to Him until we go to church. A Sunday relationship will do us no good. We have got to have fellowship with God, morning, noon and night- every day of the week.

You may be thinking, "But I don't have time to do that!"

My answer is, yes, you do. We all do. We can talk to God at any time and in any place. It's not necessary to get down on our knees and speak in religious clichés. Wherever we are, whatever we may be doing, we can talk to our heavenly Father just as we would speak to our natural father.

When you and I pray to God, He hears us. But Satan also hears us. And his number 1 job is to keep us from developing a personal relationship with the Lord. He hears what we ask of the Father, and he does his best to intercept our prayers. He tries to convince us they will never be answered. That too is part of spiritual warfare. That's why when we pray in the natural realm, we must be aware of what is going on in the spiritual realm.

In this passage, Daniel had been praying and fasting for three weeks. In the natural, nothing seemed to be happening. But then Daniel received a vision from God. An angel suddenly appeared to him. The vision was so powerful; it caused Daniel to fall to his knees with his face to the ground. Then the angel began to speak to Daniel and reveal to him what had been going on since he started praying.

YOUR PRAYER WAS HEARD!

And behold, an hand touched me, which set me upon my knees and upon the palms of my hands.

And he said unto me, O Daniel, a man greatly beloved, understand the words that I speak unto thee, and stand upright: for unto thee am I now sent. And when he had spoken this word unto me, I stood trembling.

Then said he unto me Fear not, Daniel: for from the first day that thou didst set thine heart to understand, and to chasten thyself before thy God, thy words were heard, and I am come for thy words

But the prince of the kingdom of Persia withstood me one and twenty days: but, lo, Michael, one of the chief princes, came to help me; and I remained there with the kings of Persia.

Now I am come to make thee understand what shall befall thy people in the latter days: for yet the vision is for many days.

Daniel 10:10-14

In Chapter 1 of this book, we saw there were three archangels: 1) Gabriel, the messenger of God, 2) Michael, the warrior of God, and 3) Lucifer, the worship leader for God. Here in this passage an angel has come to bring a word from the Lord to Daniel. That angel must be the archangel Gabriel, God's messenger. He touches Daniel and tells him not to fear, but to rise to his feet to hear what the Lord has to say to him.

Why does Gabriel tell Daniel not to be afraid? Because from the first day that Daniel prayed, his words were heard and God dispatched Gabriel to come and reveal to him what he asked.

But notice Gabriel's explanation of why it has taken him three weeks to arrive. He says that the prince of the kingdom of Persia- meaning a demon- withstood him.

That is spiritual warfare.

So what happened? God sent Michael, His warrior, to help Gabriel overcome the demon so he could bring Daniel the answer he had asked for of the Lord.

The angel's message was, "Daniel, from the day you prayed, God heard you and sent me to you. But I had to fight for 21 days. Now I am here with the answer to your prayer."

That should tell us that when we pray, God hears our prayers. If the answer is delayed, it may be because there is warfare going on in the heavenlies, in the spiritual realm. Gabriel, God's messenger, may be dispatched to us just as he was to Daniel. But he may have to fight his way through demons to get us and bring us and bring us our answer.

In Mark 11:24 Jesus said ... **What things soever ye desire, when ye pray, believe that ye receive them, and ye shall have them.** In John 5:14, 15 we read: **And this is the confidence that we have in him, that, if we ask any thing according to his will, he heareth us: and if we know that he hear us, whatsoever we ask, we know that we have the petitions that we desired of him.**

When you and I pray about a certain matter, we should not go back and pray for that same thing again and again. Once we have prayed, we should believe that we have received what we asked and start giving thanks to God, saying: "Father, thank You for hearing and answering my prayer. Although I don't see manifestation of it yet, I thank You because I know You have heard me and have granted me what I asked in the name of Jesus."

It may take twenty-one days or twenty-one minutes or twenty years. However long it may take, we should do as Daniel did and continue to wait on the Lord in patience and confidence, knowing that things are happening in the spiritual realm which we may not be able to perceive with our natural eye. Warfare may be taking place in the heavenlies. We do our part in that warfare by trusting God, and one way we trust God is by tithing.

The reason I stress tithing is because the only way you and I are going to be blessed is by operating by spiritual principles. Although it is challenging, when we step out in faith and obedience we move out of the natural realm and into the spiritual realm. In order to operate successfully in that realm, we must be dressed in spiritual garments.

Remember the first way to stop Satan's onslaught is to follow the directions found in Malachi 3. When we tithe, God promises to rebuke the devour for our sake and to protect our fruitful ground.

CHAPTER 5

LET'S GET DRESSED

Wherefore take unto you the whole armor of God that ye may be able to withstand in the evil day, and having done all, to stand.

Ephesians 6:13

Since we wrestle not against flesh and blood, but against powerful spiritual enemies, we must be dressed and equipped for spiritual battle. We must put on the whole armor of God so we can stand against the strategies and devices of the devil, and having done all, to stand.

Now let's examine the different pieces of our spiritual armor to see their nature and purpose.

THE BELT OF TRUTH

Stand therefore, having your loins girt about with truth....

Ephesians 6:14

In the armor of the Roman soldier, the belt was a wide leather strap that went around his waist. It was not there to hold up his pants, but to protect his loins. The word *loins* in this context refer to the lower portion of the back, one of the weakest and most sensitive parts of the human body. A strong blow to that area can break the spine and lead to paralysis.

When Paul says that we are to have our loins girt about with truth, he is telling us to make sure that the weakest part of our life is protected with the truth.

One of Satan's strongest and most effective weapon is a lie. The devil is such a deceiver he can make a lie sound like the truth. Jesus called him a liar and the father of lies. (John 8:44). But we believers have God's Word which can defeat Satan's lies.

As we have seen, each of us has certain personal weakness. It is at those weak points that the devil attacks us hardest because he knows it is there he has the greatest chance of destroying us. He comes to us and says, "If you are so holy, why don't you break that habit? If you are so strong, why don't you quit? Why have you started doing that again?"

When he attacks us with his lies, we must counterattack him with truth. We must say, "Yes, that is my weakness, but God is not through with me yet. He is still working on me, and He will strengthen me in that area."

Each of us knows our own personal sins and weaknesses. We have done things we wish we hadn't. As Paul tells us in Romans 3:23, all of us... **have sinned, and come short of the glory of God**. We must not try to deny our sin, but rather we must support it with truth. We must let the devil know, "Yes, I have sinned and come short in that area, but Jesus took care of that sin for me on the cross of Calvary."

What we must understand is that when Jesus hung on the cross in our place, He paid the price for all our sins-past, present, and future. So we no longer have to walk in guilt and condemnation, bound by the things we have done in the past.

For example, suppose a woman had an abortion in her younger days. As soon as she gets saved, the devil will try to use that memory to cause her to feel condemned. He will tell her that God can never forgive her for what she did.

That is a lie. Satan always speaks in lies, because that is his native tongue. (John 8:44). We do not have to listen to him or feel unworthy or condemned because of something that may have happened years ago. If we are saved, our sins have been washed away by the blood of Jesus, and we have been set free to live in joy and peace.

What the devil tries to do is cause us to doubt God. To resist his lies and deceptions, we need to gird on the belt of truth and stand firm against him in the power of the Lord.

THE BREASTPLATE OF RIGHTEOUSNESS

... and having on the breastplate of righteousness.

Ephesians 6:14

The breastplate covers the breast or the chest area, which includes several vital organs like the lungs and, especially, the heart.

In Proverbs 4:23 we are told, **Keep thy heart with all diligence; for out of it are the issues of life.** According to the Bible, the heart is the seat of our emotions. From it comes our sense of self-worth. That is why Satan often attacks our heart. He tries to convince us that we are not worthy of God's love and blessings.

Notice that this is the breastplate of righteousness. *Righteousness* is right standing with God. It is a symbol of His acceptance and approval.

In an effort to prove that we human beings are all unworthy creatures, people often quote Isaiah 64:6: **But we are all as an unclean thing, and all our righteousness are as filthy rags...** That was true of us in the past. Before we were saved, we were unclean, and our righteousness was as filthy rags. But now that we have come to God and been washed in the precious blood of His Son Jesus Christ, we have been cleansed of all unrighteousness and made the righteousness of God in Him. (1 John 1:9; 1 Corinthians 1:30; and 2 Corinthians 5:21).

The Bible says, **There is therefore now no condemnation to them which are in Christ Jesus, who walk not after the flesh, but after the Spirit** (Romans 8:1). Now that we are in Christ Jesus, we have God's acceptance and approval because we walk not after the flesh, but after His Spirit. If we are trying to do that which is pleasing to God, then we have on the breastplate of righteousness, so the devil has no place to get at us.

We have got to change our mentality and our self-image. We have got to learn to see ourselves approved by God. If we are in Christ Jesus, it doesn't matter what we did in the past, because now we are the righteousness of God in Jesus Christ- and that is the way He sees us.

That does not mean either that we cannot sin or that we have a license to sin. It simply means that when we do sin and come short of the glory of God, we have an Advocate to plead our case before Him. That Advocate is the Lord Jesus Christ. (1 John 2:1). The Bible says that He "even liveth" to make intercession for us with the Father. (Hebrews 7:25).

When the devil tries to accuse us and condemn us, we need to say to him, "Yes, Satan, I have made mistakes in my life. Yes, I have sinned and come short of the glory of God, but my loins are girt about with truth, and my heart is covered by the breastplate of righteousness."

With that breastplate we are able to protect our heart, from which flow the issues of life. Why is the heart so important? Because, as Jesus has told us, it is out of the abundance of the heart the mouth speaks. (Matthew 12:34). And it is by our spoken words that we are either justified or condemned. (Matthew 12:37).

Whatever we fill our heart with will come out of our mouth. That's why it is so important to fill our heart with the Word of God and to protect it with the breastplate of righteousness.

THE SHOES OF THE GOSPEL

And your feet shod with the preparation of the gospel of peace. - Ephesians 6:5

So we are to put on the belt of truth and the breastplate of righteousness, but as long as we are barefoot we are still not fully dressed.

A woman can buy the most beautiful dress in the world, but if she tries to go out into public wearing that dress without the shoes that go with it she will not be properly attired.

Most men are amazed to find how particular women are about the perfect pair of shoes. She may have 5 pairs of black shoes in her closet, but nothing to wear with her black dress. It requires the right pair of shoes.

Shoes have a greater mission than simply looking good, however. They offer protection for the part of the body bearing the weight. The right shoes protect feet from scrapes, cuts, disease, and stubbed toes.

Proper shoes are critical for protection from pain that could cripple the entire body. What shoes go with the belt of truth and the breastplate of righteousness? The shoes of preparation of the Gospel of peace.

What is the Gospel? It is good news. Good news about what? Good news about the death, burial, and resurrection of Jesus Christ.

Jesus, the Son of God, came to this earth to redeem mankind and to save us from our sins. He lived, died, rose again, ascended into heaven, and will one day come again to receive unto Himself all those who are waiting and looking for His return. That is the Gospel, the good news of peace that we are to share with others.

Isaiah 52:7 says, **How beautiful upon the mountains are the feet of him that bringeth good tidings, that publisheth peace; that bringeth good tidings of good, that publisheth salvation; that saith unto Zion, Thy God reigneth!**

As the sons and daughters of God, we must be bearers of those good tidings. We must always be prepared to share the good news – in season and out of season (2 Timothy 4:2) – everywhere our feet may take us. Wherever we go – to church, to the mall, to the office or the classroom – we should go prepared to spread the good news of what God has done for us on Jesus Christ. (Luke 8:39).

We may not be able to quote a lot of Scriptures. We may not be able to deliver a homiletically structured sermon. But we can all share with others what God has done in our lives. That is enough to lead someone else out of the darkness and into the Kingdom of God. (Colossians 1:13). All we have to do is have our feet shod with the willingness and the preparation to share the good news of Jesus Christ with those around us.

THE SHIELD OF FAITH

Above all, taking the shield of faith, wherewith ye shall be able to quench all the fiery darts of the wicked.

Ephesians 6:16

What is the purpose of a shield? It is to turn away attacks. Paul says that the devil is shooting fiery darts at us. Often those darts take the form of lies. When people lie about us, their words are like darts aimed at our heart. We are to turn them away by holding up the shield faith.

The same is true for worries and cares. To many rich people their god is their wealth. On Sunday morning they are not in church; they are out on the golf course or riding around in their yacht – because that is where their faith is. But for all their money, they are in danger, because they are putting their trust in gold rather than in God.

We believers may not have the material wealth that others enjoy, but we have something much better – our faith. It is true we may not have every material possession we would like, but we have something much more precious and enduring – the Word of the Lord. Our Father in heaven has promised to meet our every need, if we are faithful to Him. That's why I teach and will continue to teach about the importance of the tithe.

In Malachi 3:10 the Lord says to us: **Bring ye all the tithes into the storehouse, that there may be meat in**

**mine house, and prove me now herewith, saith the
LORD of hosts, if I will not open you the windows of
heaven, and pour you out a blessing, that there shall not
be room enough to receive it.** And Psalm 84:11 tells us
that... **the Lord God is a sun and shield: the Lord will
give grace and glory: no good thing will he withhold
from them that walk uprightly.**

God has promised us if we will be obedient to Him,
He will meet our every need, as we read in Philippians
4:19...**God shall supply all your need according to his
riches in glory by Christ Jesus.** Obedience is evidence of
faith. When we believe, we obey. It's just that simple.

Many people are not being obedient to God in
regard to their money because they think if they give Him
10 percent of it, they will not have enough left to meet their
own needs. That is fear, and it comes from Satan.

Jesus has told us that God knows what we need.
(Matthew 6:8). Our heavenly Father knows we need money
to pay our bills and but food and clothes for ourselves and
our family. That's why He says to us, "Prove Me." What
He means is, "Put Me to the test. Try Me and see if I won't
meet your every need, just as I have promised in My
Word." The way we put the Lord to the test is by operating
in faith rather than in fear.

FAITH VERSUS FEAR

I will lift up mine eyes unto the hills, from whence cometh my help.

My help cometh from the Lord, which made heaven and earth.

He will not suffer thy foot to be moved: he that keepeth thee will not slumber.

Behold, he that keepeth Israel shall neither slumber nor sleep.

The Lord is thy keeper...

The Lord shall preserve thee from all evil: he shall preserve thy soul.

Psalm 121:1-5, 7

The opposite of faith is not doubt, it is fear. The psalmist said that he did not fear, because his faith and trust were in his Keeper, the God of Israel Who neither slumbers nor sleeps.

Paul did not say, "Take up the shield of *fear*," but "Take up the shield of *faith*." That simply means trusting God in spite of the way things may appear.

I know there are a lot of things going on in our world today to cause fear. Our church is located in New

Orleans, Louisiana, which has one of the highest homicide rates in the nation. In some areas of the city it seems there are killings taking place constantly. But in His Word, God has promised to protect and keep those who put their trust and confidence in Him.

In Psalm 91:5, 6 we are told, **Thou shalt not be afraid for the terror by night.... nor for the pestilence that walketh in darkness...**

I know of people in our city who sleep with all of the lights on their house because they are afraid. The devil is attacking their finances by deceiving them into wasting hundreds of dollars a year on electricity bills. They need to turn their lights off and go to sleep – because God has promised to stay awake and watch out for us.

In Psalm 91:9-11 the psalmist tell us: **Because thou hast made the LORD, which is my refuge, even the most High, thy habitation; there shall no evil befall thee, neither shall any plague come nigh thy dwelling. For he shall give his angels charge over thee, to keep thee in all thy ways.**

That does not mean that we can sleep on the front porch with the doors open. There is a difference between faith and foolishness. It is wisdom to go inside at night and lock our doors and windows. But it does mean that we believers are to live in faith, not fear.

Today many people are victims of what I call the "fear syndrome." They are afraid of the dark, afraid of storms, afraid of crime, afraid of losing their job, afraid of catching some dreaded disease, afraid of heights, and on and on. Some people are so afraid of flying they won't get on an airplane. Instead they will take a train – which many times is just as dangerous – and spend days getting somewhere they could have reached in a matter of hours.

In 2 Timothy 1:7 the Apostle Paul tells us that…**God hath not given us the spirit of fear; but of power, and of love, and of a sound mind.** Fear is a spirit, and it must be countered by the spiritual weapon – the shield of faith.

OVERCOMING SETBACKS

The steps of a good man are ordered by the Lord: and he delighteth in his way.

Though he fall, he shall not be utterly cast down: for the Lord upholdeth him with his hand.

Psalm 37:23, 24

Many people have gone through serious trials in their lifetime. You may be one of them. You may have experienced a discouraging setback in your life. If so, let me give you a word from the Lord: *A setback is a setup for a comeback.*

You must understand that everything that has happened to you to this point has been for a reason. God allowed you to go through those experiences for a purpose. He was leading you to the place you are right now. He was ordering your steps so He could delight in your way. Even though you may have fallen, you have not been totally cast down, because God has been upholding you by His mighty hand.

Despite what has happened to you, God still has plans for you, as He promises in Jeremiah 29:11: **For I know the thoughts that I think toward you, saith the Lord, thoughts of peace, and not of evil, to give you an expected end.** Whatever you may have experienced in the past, don't be afraid or discouraged, because God is not through with you yet.

I don't know why we must go through hard times. But I do know that those hard times are either sent by God or are allowed by Him to bring us where we need to be. Faced with the past, we must do what Paul said he did:... **this one thing I do, forgetting those things which are behind, and reaching forth unto those things which are before, I press toward the mark for the prize of the high calling of God in Christ Jesus** (Philippians 3:13,14).

As we continue to press toward the mark of God's high calling upon us, the devil will try to hinder us by shooting at us fiery darts – darts of doubt and fear, darts of regret and remorse, darts of condemnation and unworthiness. Whatever you have gone through in your life

91

up to this point, put it behind you. Don't let the devil keep you from trusting God. Lift up against him the shield of faith and the weapon of praise.

As we have seen, praise is a spiritual weapon, but it only works if it is used. When things start to go wrong in your daily life, begin to praise the Lord, because as the song says, 'When praises go up, blessing come down."

THE HELMET OF SALVATION

And take the helmet of salvation...

Ephesians 6:17

The helmet is to protect the head, which is the seat of the mind. In Philippians 2:5 we are told by Paul, **Let this mind be in you, which was also in Christ Jesus.** In other words, Paul is telling us that we need to protect our thoughts.

As believers, the devil sends thoughts into our head that are not in keeping with the Word of God. That's why we must have within us the mind of Christ.

In that same letter to the Philippians, Paul goes on to say: **Finally, brethren, whatsoever things are true, whatsoever things are honest, whatsoever things are just, whatsoever things are pure, whatsoever things are lovely, whatsoever things are of good report; if there be**

any virtue, and if there be any praise, think on these things. (Philippians 4:8).

Why do we have to think on all these things? Because if we don't keep our mind filled with good thoughts, the devil will send into it all kinds of evil thoughts.

Once you and I are saved by putting our faith and trust in the Lord Jesus Christ, the challenge is not that we have to learn so many new things, but that we have to forget so many old things. Our task as Christians is not so much learning as unlearning.

Before we are saved, if someone insulted us, what did we do? We gave that person a piece of our mind. But now that we belong to Christ, our job is to give other people a piece of His mind.

Remember, the devil's number one objective is to make us doubt God. One way he does that is by placing questions in our mind. Do you remember what the serpent said to Eve in the Garden of Eden: ... **Yea, hath God said...?** (Genesis 3:1). That is the same kind of question he puts into our mind.

For example, take the verse we saw in Malachi 3 about the tithe in which God promises to open the windows of heaven and pour out blessings on those who give a tenth of their income to Him. The devil will whisper in our ears, "You don't really believe that, do you? It doesn't make sense. How are you going to have more money coming in by putting more money out?"

Satan wants us to doubt God, because he knows if he can get us to do that, he can keep us limited in our lives. That's why he tries to convince us that acting in obedience to God's Word does not work.

Suppose we are praying for the salvation of a loved one. The devil hears our prayer and tempts that loved one into acting worse than ever before. What Satan is trying to do is convince us that prayer does not work.

The devil also tries to keep us from thinking on the things of God by keeping our thoughts on the things we need or fear or hate. That's why our mind needs to be renewed in accordance with the Word of God.

RENEWING THE MIND

I beseech you therefore, brethren, by the mercies of God, that ye present your bodies a living sacrifice, holy, acceptable unto God, which is your reasonable service.

And be not conformed to this world: but be ye transformed by the renewing of your mind, that ye may prove what is that good, and acceptable, and perfect, will of God.

Romans 12:1, 2

We have got to renew our mind on a daily basis. When a thought comes to us, we must ask ourselves where it came from. There are only two possible sources: God and Satan. If a thought is not true, honest, just, pure, lovely, of good report, virtuous, or praiseworthy, then it is not from God, so we can know where it came from.

The problem is that when we have a thought, too often we speak it forth out of our mouth without considering what we are saying. We need to test our thoughts. If they are not in line with the Word of God, we must cast them down and bring them into captivity, into obedience to Christ – which is another form of spiritual warfare.

CASTING DOWN IMAGINATIONS

(For the weapons of our warfare are not carnal, but mighty through God to pulling down of strong holds;)

Casting down imaginations, and every high thing that exalteth itself against the knowledge of God, and bringing into captivity every thought to the obedience of Christ.

2 Corinthians 10:4, 5

If a thought occurs in our mind which we recognize as coming from Satan, what are we to do? We are to cast it down. We are to say, "Satan, I do not receive that thought, because it's a lie." How can we know it's a lie? We can know it's a lie because everything Satan says is a lie.

The trouble with entertaining a negative thought is that it develops into an imagination, which sooner or later exalts itself against the knowledge of God.

In Genesis 6 the Lord decided to wipe from the face of the earth every human being except Noah and his family. Why? Because... **God saw that the wickedness of man was great in the earth, and that every imagination of the thoughts of his heart was only evil continually.** (v.5)

That's why it is so important that we keep our mind on things of God and cast down the evil thoughts that come to us from Satan who tries to get us to doubt the Lord.

In 2 Corinthians 5:17 we read, **Therefore if any man be in Christ, he is a new creature: old things are passed away; behold, all things are become new.** Since we are new creatures in Christ, we have got to develop new patterns of thought. We have got to renew our mind daily, so it is attuned to the things of God and not to the things of the world. We must put on the helmet of salvation to protect our mind from the attacks of the enemy.

THE SWORD OF THE SPIRIT

And take... the sword of the Spirit, which is the word of God.

Ephesians 6:17

Notice that the sword of the Spirit is the only offensive weapon mentioned in this list of the armor of God. All of the other pieces – the belt of truth, the breastplate of righteousness, the shoes of preparation of the Gospel of peace, the shield of faith, and the helmet of salvation – are designed to protect us against the enemy. But God wants us not only to be protected against the devil, but also to do him some damage.

For too long Satan has been doing damage to the Body of Christ. Now it is time for Christians to take up the sword of the Spirit and go after the devil.

For too long the Church of Jesus Christ has been backing up while the devil has been running rampant against it and through it. The Church has been dying for years. In many churches, nothing is happening. Nobody is getting saved or healed or blessed. I believe God is raising up a people who are taking His Word and using it against the enemy to take back what rightfully belongs to them.

Our church, Beacon Light Baptist Church, gives all the glory to God for the fact that is the talk of the town. We are happy and excited because God is adding to us more people and more services. We are grateful to the Lord that we have to bring in extra chairs for our Bible studies because there is not enough seating for all those who want to attend.

But we are wise enough to know that the devil is not happy and excited about that. We know he is planning and scheming, plotting what to do to stop this mighty move of God in our midst.

What the Lord has revealed to us is what we shared in the beginning of this book: "My people are destroyed for lack of knowledge." The reason they are being destroyed is that they have failed to put on the whole armor of God and take up the sword of the Spirit, which is the Word of God.

The way the Church of Jesus Christ can stand against the devil and his wiles is by growing in the Word. We have seen that faith comes by hearing, and hearing by the Word of God. That is the only offensive weapon we have against our spiritual enemy. The sword of the Spirit is not to be kept in our pocket. We are to take it out and use it against the devil.

For too long the Church has been on the defensive. Now God is raising up a people who are going to do some damage to the devil and his demons. It is time for us believers to start taking the offensive.

In James 4:7 we are told, **Submit yourselves therefore to God. Resist the devil, and he will flee from you.** It confuses the devil when we resist him, when we take a stand against him and praise God even in the very midst of his attacks against us. Satan is not prepared for us to use the weapon of praise. He is use to us just lying down and taking his abuse.

So often when we ask people how things are going, they answer, "Oh, the devil's been busy!" Yes, the devil is on his job. Now it's time for the Church of Jesus Christ to get on their job. And our job is take on the armor of God and take up the sword of the Spirit, which is the Word of God, and start doing battle against the enemy, confident that as we resist him he will flee from us. One important way we wield that sword is through prayer, which is itself a powerful spiritual instrument.

CHAPTER 6

THE MISSING LINK

Praying always with all prayer and supplication in the Spirit, and watching thereunto with all perseverance and supplication for all saints.

Ephesians 6:18

We have seen that in the army the frontline fighting troops are divided into different- sized groups called platoons, companies, battalions, and so forth. Behind the front lines are the support sections. One of these is the supply sections, which provides the food, clothing, ammunition, and other material needed by the fighting units. Without these vital supplies, the army cannot do its job.

As soldiers of the cross, our Source is God. In His Word, He has promised to provide us everything we need to carry on our battle against the enemy. (Philippians 4:19). The way we requisition those supplies is through prayer as we see in Matthew 7:7, 8 in which Jesus said, **Ask, and it shall be given you; seek, and ye shall find; knock, and it shall be opened unto you: for every one that asketh receiveth; and he that seeketh findeth; and to him that knocketh it shall be opened.**

If we are to be successful in our campaign against the enemy, we must constantly make requisitions from our supply section, but we must also keep in close communication with our Commander.

The "Commo Section"

If any of you lack wisdom, let him ask of God, that giveth to all men liberally, and upbraideth not; and it shall be given him.

James 1:5

There is another rear-echelon support group called the "commo section," which is short for the communication section. It doesn't matter how many troops, rifles, machine guns, tanks, grenades, and rocket launchers there are on the front lines, without proper communication the battle will be lost.

One reason many Christians are being defeated today is that they are trying to fight the enemy without proper communication.

Yes, we must put on our armor for protection. Yes, we must take up and use our offensive weapon, which is the sword of the Spirit, the Word of God. Yes, we must requisition the supplies and ammunition we need to carry on the battle. But we must also stay in close contact with the "commo section" if we are to know what the enemy is doing and how to best attack and defeat him. How do we do that? Through prayer.

There are many Christians who talk a lot about prayer, but who do very little actual praying. Prayer is the missing link in the average believer's life. The truth is that the level of our spiritual development will never rise any higher than our level of prayer.

How can we say we love our spouse if we never communicate with him or her? In the same way, how can we confess that we love the Lord with our whole heart and mind and soul, and yet never spend more than five minutes communicating with Him?

The more we communicate with another person, the better we get to know that individual. The devil is aware of the fact. That's why he tries so hard to keep us from communicating with God. He sees it as his job to keep us so busy we never have time for prayer. One reason we seldom do the enemy any damage is because we are not in touch with our "commo section"

Notice in Ephesians 6:18 that we are to pray always. One way to do that is to make quick, brief prayers our habitual response to every situation.

In my case, I have developed my prayer life to such a degree that prayer is now a habit. When something comes up and I don't have time to make a long, formal prayer, I simply pray, "Help me, Lord!" At other times I may only have time to pray, "In the name of Jesus!" There are some instances when I only have time for "LORD!"

As believers, prayer must become so much a part of our nature and attitude that whatever happens to us, we respond instantly with a blessing instead of a curse. No matter what the situation we may be in, we can almost always find time to offer a prayer of thanksgiving to God for the blessing we have rather than bemoaning the things we don't have.

When we are waiting for a bus, instead of getting jealous and envious of those who pass by in big expensive cars, we can say, "Thank You, Lord, that I have bus fare."

Once we get on the bus to go to our job, instead of complaining about having to work so hard, we can thank God that we have a job to go to – especially when we pass by the unemployment office and see all those people standing in line trying to get work.

By making prayer a habit, we actually make it a lifestyle. We become so accustomed to praying instant prayers that our very lifestyle becomes a prayer. In order to pray, we don't have to isolate ourselves from others or from our daily routine or work. We can be standing on the assembly line or sitting at the computer and say, "Lord, I thank You and praise You for the growth that is taking place in my life."

Whatever our situation or circumstance, we can spend time talking to the Lord. When we draw close to God, He draws close to us. (James 4:8). The more faithful we are to Him, the more faithful He is to us.

As soldiers of the cross, we are to put on the armor of God, take up the sword of the Spirit, which is the Word of God, and keep in constant communication with our Commander-in-Chief.

THE POWER OF PRAYER

... The effectual fervent prayer of a righteous man availeth much.

James 5:16

In the last chapters we are examining the most effective of all spiritual weapons, which is prayer. As we have seen, prayer is powerful. But the voice tone used in prayer has absolutely nothing to do with its effectiveness. Some of us Christians seem to think that if we pray loud enough, we will have power with God. That is not so. In fact, some of our most powerful prayers are silent, those in which we say nothing at all.

Too often, especially in public prayers, we seem to think we will appear more spiritual if we pray at the top of our voice. Again, that is untrue. If you and I want to be able to pray powerful prayers, we must establish and maintain a personal relationship with the living God.

Prayer power is not produced by religion, but by relationship.

More than anything else, God wants to have relationship with His children. He wants us to know that we are kin to Him, that we are part of His family. He also wants us to enjoy fellowship and companionship together.

When we are close to someone, we want to be with that individual. We want to communicate with that person on a very deep and intimate level. The same is true of God. Because of our relationship, He wants us to be in close contact with one another.

The result of relationship, fellowship, companionship, and communication with God is power in prayer, as we see in the book of Acts.

PRINCIPLES OF POWERFUL PRAYER

And... they lifted up their voice to God with one accord, and said, Lord, thou art God, which hast made heaven, and earth, and the sea, and all that in them is:

Who by the mouth of thy servant David hast said, Why did the heathen rage, and the people imagine vain things?

The kings of the earth stood up, and the rulers were gathered together against the Lord, and against his Christ.

For of a truth against thy holy child Jesus, whom thou hast anointed, both Herod, and Pontius Pilate, with the Gentiles, and the people of Israel, were gathered together,

For to do whatsoever thy hand and thy counsel determined before to be done.

And now, Lord, behold their threatening: and grant unto thy servants, that with all boldness they may speak thy word,

By stretching forth thine hand to heal; and that signs and wonders may be done by the name of thy holy child Jesus.

And when they had prayed, the place was shaken where they were assembled together; and they were all filled with the Holy Ghost, and they spake the word of God with boldness.

Acts 4:24-31

In this passage and the following verses there are some important principles we learn from the disciples' prayer experience.

As we have seen, power in prayer is based on relationship with God. Because the disciples were aware of the relationship between God and His Son Jesus Christ, and between God and them, they were able to pray powerful prayers that shook the very foundations of their world and made them effective witnesses for the Lord.

We have also seen that powerful prayer is the result of time spent in the presence of God. That's why the devil tries to interfere with our prayer time. Because he knows the power of prayer, Satan tries to keep us so busy we don't have time to pray.

Finally, powerful prayer depends upon acknowledging God as the One Who made heaven and earth and the sea and everything in the midst of it. That is the 1st principle of prayer we will consider.

1. Recognize God as Creator

If you and I are to pray powerful prayers, we must learn to look beyond the creature to the Creator of all things and of all people. We must not allow ourselves to be affected by what is going on in our lives at the moment. We must not get all down and depressed because of problems between us and our boss or our co-workers or our family members. We must keep our eyes on God, not on ourselves and our circumstances or situations.

A good way to keep our focus on the Lord and His power rather than on ourselves and our problems is to begin our prayer by saying: "Lord, I thank You that You created all things and all people. You have made us, and not we ourselves. You are the One Who sustains us and takes care of us, so we entrust ourselves entirely into Your keeping."

As we go through our day, we can continue to pray, thanking God for each wonderful thing He has provided for us to enjoy and every person He has brought into our lives to enrich it. Like the psalmist, we can give Him continual thanks for the bounty of the earth and the marvels of the heavens. We can thank Him for the blessing of marriage and family and friendship – for wisdom and truth and beauty, for life and all the good things in it.

The Lord loves to hear His children recount to Him all His blessing to them and give Him thanks for what He has done and praise for Who He is. He already knows Who He is, but He still likes to hear it from us, because it shows that we recognize His majesty and power and appreciate His goodness and mercy toward us.

That's what the disciples did here in this passage. They gave credit to God for Who He is and for all that He has done as Creator. That's one reason their prayer was so powerful. Another reason their prayer was so effective is that they recognized God as Controller.

2. Recognize God as Controller

Once we come to recognize God as Creator, we must come to recognize Him as Controller. God is sovereign, meaning that not only did He create the universe, but that He does whatever He wants to with it, whenever He wants to do it.

Once we come to see the majesty and power of Almighty God, we are no longer, so concerned about what other people may think or say or do or about what might happen in the future.

Notice what the disciples said about God in verses 25-28 of Acts, chapter 4: **Who by the mouth of thy servant David hast said, Why did the heathen rage, and the people imagine vain things? The kings of the earth**

stood up, and the rulers were gathered together against the Lord, and against his Christ. For of a truth against **thy holy child Jesus, whom thou hast anointed, both Herod, and Pontius Pilate, with the Gentiles, and the people of Israel, were gathered together,** *for to do whatsoever thy hand and thy counsel determined before to be done.*

In this prayer the disciples were quoting from Psalm 2:1, 2: **Why do the heathen rage and the people imagine a vain thing? The kings of the earth set themselves, and the rulers take counsel together, against the Lord, and against his anointed...**

What the disciples were doing was seeing the fulfillment of this prophecy in their own day. They had seen Jesus brought before Herod and Pontius Pilate. They had seen Him despised, rejected, and crucified for the sins of the whole world. They recognized that everything that had taken place was in accordance with the plan and purpose of God Who had been in control of the entire situation from beginning to end.

What you and I need to learn from this passage is that whatever may happen to us, God is still in charge. Although we may have problems, God is still our Creator and Controller of our lives.

Whatever we may experience in this life, God is still on his throne. That knowledge should help us. We should be able to face our problems and pray, "Lord, You are my Creator and my Controller. You know what is happening in my life and why. You have a plan for me, and You will work out everything for my good."

No matter what we may be facing or experiencing on this earth, there is no reason to panic. Because there is no panic in heaven, only plans.

God never calls an emergency session of the Holy Trinity to discuss what's going on in our lives. He never asks Jesus or the Holy Spirit, "What are we going to do about this terrible situation down there on earth?" God is not the One Who panics; we are the ones who panic. The reason we panic is that we do not know the Lord's plan.

We have got to understand that everything we face or go through in this life, both good and bad, is part of God's plan to get us from where we are to where He wants us to be. Just as the heavenly Father had a plan for Jesus, so He has a plan for each one of us. Our job is to do as Jesus did and cooperate with God's plan, so we can reap the blessings it will produce in the end.

The reason the Holy Trinity never has to meet in emergency session is that each of the Persons of the Godhead already knows the outcome.

We must realize that everything we will experience in our lifetime – from dropping a fork on the kitchen floor to being diagnosed with cancer – has been known to God from the foundation of the world. Absolutely none of it will catch God by surprise. It should help us to face trying times, knowing that whatever may happen, God is saying to us, "Don't worry, I'm in control of this situation."

In Psalm 37:23 we saw that the steps of a good man are ordered by the Lord. That means that although we may have gone through some hard times in the past, and may have to go through some hard times in the future, it is all just as much a part of God's plan for our benefit as the trials Jesus had to endure were part of God's plan for our salvation.

In their prayer, the disciples said that everything that happened to Jesus was done in accordance with God's counsel and plan. The reason God gave His approval to what His enemies were about to do to His Son was that He knew the outcome of it before it ever took place.

The same is true for us as God's children. God knows what is going to happen to us, and He has already made plans to bring a blessing out of it: And we know that all things work together for good to them that love God, to them who are the called according to His purpose (Romans 8:28). Whatever happened to us, God has a plan and a purpose for it, just as He did in what happened to Jesus.

The Bible speaks of two gardens: The Garden of Eden and the Garden of Gethsemane. The Garden of Eden is mentioned in the book of Genesis. The Garden of Gethsemane is mentioned by name in the gospels of Matthew and Mark. But despite their order in the Bible, the Garden of Gethsemane came before the Garden of Eden.

Of course, Gethsemane is the place where Jesus went to pray just before His arrest, trial, and crucifixion. It was in the Garden of Gethsemane that Jesus' sweat became like great drops of the blood as He faced what He was about to suffer for the sins of the world. (Luke 22:44). It was there that He prayed to His heavenly Father, "Not My will, but Yours, be done." (Luke 22:42).

The Garden of Eden was created first by God, because that is where He placed Adam and Eve. But because God knew from the beginning that Adam and Eve were going to sin, He had already made plans for Jesus to come and suffer and die to redeem them from their sin.

Before the serpent ever deceived Adam and Eve into eating of the tree of the knowledge of good and evil, God had already made His plan of redemption, which included Jesus and His sacrifice on the cross of Calvary.

Now let's make that personal. Whatever you and I are going through right now, God has known about it from before the foundation of the world, and He already has the solution to it. All we have to do is go through the process necessary to discover what that solution is.

Before Adam and Eve ever sinned, God had planned and prepared for Jesus to come to the earth to purchase their redemption. How do we know that? In John 1:1-3 we read: **In the beginning was the Word, and the Word was with God, and the Word was God. The same was in the beginning with God. All things were made by him; and without him was not anything made that was made.**

Since Jesus is the Word mentioned here, that means that He was there at the beginning and participated in creation.

In Genesis 1:26 when God said, ...**Let us make man in our image, after our likeness**..., Who was He speaking of? He was speaking of the Trinity – Father, Son, and Holy Spirit. Since Jesus is the Word of God Who took part in creation, and since He is the Second Person of the Trinity, He was there before Adam and Eve were created – and before they sinned and needed a Savior.

God knew what was going to happen to the man and woman before they were created. He planned for Jesus to come to this earth and suffer death on the cross for their redemption. Therefore, the Garden of Gethsemane was planned by God before the Garden of Eden.

What does that mean for us and our life with God? It means that before anything happens to us, God knows it already. He has known it from before the foundation of the world. And He has made a plan to take care of it, just as he did for Adam and Eve.

If we know God as Creator and Controller, it is hard for us to be defeated in any situation that may arise. That knowledge is what helps us to live victoriously on a daily basis. No matter what may happen to us, there is always that still small voice that whispers in our ear, "Don't worry about it. I'm still in control. Don't panic. It's all part of the plan. Just trust Me, and it will all turn out for good, because you are called according to My purpose."

But notice that God's plan work only for those who are called according to His purpose – that is, those who are committed to Him.

3. Recognize prayer must be support by commitment.

The reason many of us have not been able to deal successfully with our problems is that we have not been totally committed to the Lord. Part of the problem has been our false image of God. It is hard to have confidence in a God Whom we see as sitting on a throne ready to punish us every time we mess up. We have got to learn that God is not like that, that He gets no pleasure in punishing us just because we are less than perfect.

The disciples did not have that view of God. They saw Him as ready to intervene and help them, as we see in Acts 4:29, 30 in which they prayed: **And now, Lord,**

behold their threatening: and grant unto thy servants, that with all boldness they may speak thy word, by stretching forth thine hand to heal; and that signs and wonders may be done by the name of thy holy child Jesus.

Now they did not say, "Grant unto Thy members," or "Thy deacons," or "Thy choir members," or "Thy church board." Instead, they said, "Grant unto Thy servants." In this context a *servant* is a slave, one who is totally sold out to God.

The problem for some of us is that we are trying to hold relationships in both worlds. We want to fellowship with God on Sunday and with the devil the rest of the week. If we expect the Lord to be on our side, then we are going to have to be on His side.

Answered prayer is not for rebels, for unbelievers, and not for those who are disobedient. It is for the faithful, the believers, and for those who are obedient to the Lord and His Word. That does not mean we have to be perfect, it just means that we have to be committed to God.

Judging by their prayer, there were three things these servants of the Lord really desired:

First, they wanted to express God's Word. Although they were already in trouble for speaking that Word and acting on it, they were asking God to help them be more effective witnesses.

116

Second, they wanted to extend the hand of God. They were asking Him to stretch forth His hand to heal and perform signs and wonders in the name of His Son Jesus Christ. What they were really saying was, "Lord, allow our mouths to become Your mouth, our hands to become Your hands. Whatever You want to do in the earth realm, do it through us."

God obviously answered their prayer because in the next chapter we read: **And by the hands of the apostles were many signs and wonders wrought among the people; (and they were all with one accord....) (Acts 5:12).**

These people were truly concerned about those who were not as blessed as they were. That's why they were such good intercessors, which is what we all need to be, as we will see in the final chapter of this book. If you and I will pray for others with the same intensity that these people did, God will honor our prayers just as He honored theirs.

Third, they wanted to bring glory to God. Their prayer was not that they would be glorified, but that the Lord would glorify Himself by performing signs and wonders through the name of His Son Jesus Christ.

If we want our prayers answered, we must learn to seek God's will and His glory more than our own. Not all of us can be apostles, prophets, evangelist, pastors, and teachers, as we read in Ephesians 4:11, but we can all be witnesses. We don't have to go around with a big Bible under our arm or a huge cross hanging from our neck for other people to recognize that we are believers. People should be able to tell that we are Christians by our everyday lives and by the way we behave among them day by day. There should be something different about us, something that attracts them and makes them want to know more about us and our Lord.

We don't need to talk in religious clichés to call attention to ourselves and our relationship with God. We can do that by our very being. That doesn't mean that we are to act like or think that we are better than everybody else just because we Christians. But what it does mean is that we should be revealed by our attitude and actions that we belong to Jesus Christ.

That is what the disciples did. They asked God to stretch forth His hands and heal and work signs and wonders through them. Not so others would say, "Oh, those are powerful people!", but so God would be glorified.

In our church in New Orleans, it is not our vision just to grow and add more worship services to our weekly schedule. That's not what we are all about. Our goal is to lift up Jesus because He has said that if He is lifted up, He will draw all men to Himself. (John 12:32).

We didn't go out and buy a van, so we can print BEACON LIGHT BAPTIST CHURCH on its side in big letters and drive it up and down the streets for people to see. We bought it so we could use it for the glory of God.

The more we give of ourselves to others, the more they will see God in us, and the more He will be glorified through us. That's why we should all be tithers. Not so the Church can stack up a pile of money, but so the Church can have the funds it needs to do the work of the Lord by ministering to others.

God has promised that if we will tithe; He will open the windows of heaven and pour out upon us such a blessing that there will not be room enough to receive it. That is a promise from the Lord. And God keeps His promises, as we see when these people prayed in accordance with His will, asking that His Word be expressed, His hand extended, and His name glorified.

PRAYER AS COMMUNION

And the multitude of them that believed were of one heart and of one soul: neither said any of them that ought of the things which he possessed was his own; but they had all things common.

And with great power gave the apostles witness of the resurrection of the Lord Jesus: and great grace was upon them all.

Acts 4:32, 33

119

These people got their prayers answered because they not only knew God as Creator and Controller, but also because they knew that prayer must be supported by commitment. They also knew that they needed God's grace upon them on a daily basis. That's why they prayed in the name of Jesus.

A person's name reflects his character. Just because we end a prayer with the phrase "in Jesus' name" does not mean it is a powerful prayer or that it will be answered. The name of Jesus was never meant to be a tag added to the end of a prayer. It was meant to carry power and authority.

When we ask God for something in Jesus' name, we are doing what the disciples did in their prayer. We are asking God to stretch forth His hand and act in response to our request by all the power and authority that is resident in the name of His Son Jesus Christ, so that He will receive all the glory.

The thing that moves God is faith, the expectation that He will do something, so that His will may be accomplished and His name may be glorified. More than anything, God wants glory in the earth realm. That's why we should pray daily that the words we speak are words He wants spoken and the things we do are the things He wants done – for His glory not ours.

If we want to pray powerful prayers, we must want God to receive glory. And one way He does that is by bringing us through the trials and tribulations that the devil brings upon us. Satan is constantly causing us problems in this life. But the good new news is God delivers the righteous out of *all* his or her afflictions. (Psalm 34:9).

Notice that the prayer of the disciples was answered when they asked *in one accord*. It was when they were all assembled together in prayer that the place was shaken on its foundations, and they were filled with the presence and power of the Holy Spirit, so they spoke God's Word with boldness.

Powerful prayer is based on communion

As we have seen, true prayer is based on relationship, not religion. Just because we are in church Sunday after Sunday does not mean that we are in close fellowship with the Lord or with one another.

God doesn't want us coming to Him in prayer only when we have problems. He doesn't appreciate being treated like a spare tire that we get out only when we run into trouble and then ignore the rest of the time. Our heavenly Father wants to enjoy fellowship and companionship with us every day of our lives.

If we want our prayers to be powerful, we need to be in constant communion with God and with each other, lifting up one another before His throne of grace.

CHAPTER 7

STANDING IN THE GAP

I exhort therefore, that first of all, supplications, prayers, intercessions, and giving of thanks, be made for all men.

1 Timothy 2:1

You and I can have on every piece of our spiritual armor and be armed with all of our spiritual weapons, but if we don't establish an accurate prayer life we will still be defeated.

Statistics have shown that the average Christian spends about seven minutes a week in prayer. How can any army expect to be successful if it spends so little time in communication with its commander?

We must understand that intercessory prayer is one of the most powerful instruments of spiritual warfare. When we go before the Lord and pray about a particular issue, we get God involved in it. That's why our enemy tries so hard to keep us from praying. That's also why it is so important that we understand intercessory prayer.

INTERCESSION DEFINED

And I sought for a man among them, that should make up the hedge, and stand in the gap before me for the land... but I found none.

Ezekiel 22:30

I once asked a gathering of Christians if any of them knew what intercessory prayer was, and only about 45 percent of them raised their hands to say yes. That is average. But it is a sad commentary on the situation in many Christian churches today. No wonder most of us believers are such ineffective spiritual warriors.

Simply stated, *intercession* is the act of praying for someone else. In biblical times, to intercede is to "make up the hedge" "or stand in the gap," meaning to go before God on behalf of someone other than ourselves.

Each of us is a beneficiary of intercessory prayer. Whether we are aware of it or not, we are where we are today because someone else prayed for us. We are all the fruit of intercession.

As we have seen in Hebrews 7:25, Jesus Christ Himself, "ever liveth" to make intercession for us. In Romans 8:26, 27 we also see that the Holy Spirit makes intercession for us: **Likewise the Spirit also helpeth our infirmities: for we know not what we should pray for as we ought: but the Spirit itself maketh intercession for us with groanings which cannot be uttered. And he that searcheth the hearts knoweth what is the mind of the Spirit, because he maketh intercession for the saints according to the will of God.** The Holy Spirit prays for us according to the will of God for us. The will of God for us is that we pray for one another and for others, including those in authority.

PRAYER FOR THOSE IN AUTHORITY

For kings, and for all that are in authority; that we may lead a quiet and peaceable life in all godliness and honesty.

For this is good and acceptable in the sight of God our Savior.

1 Timothy 2:2,3

In 1 Timothy 2:1, The Apostle Paul wrote to exhort that supplications, prayers, intercessions, and giving of thanks be made for all men – meaning for all people. In verses 2 and 3 he went on to urge that intercession be made for all of those in authority.

As the sons and daughters of God, it is our job to intercede not only for one another, but also for others – including those in positions of power over us.

Too often we hear Christians murmuring and complaining about their elected officials from the local city alderman all the way up to the president of the United States.

If we are not pleased with the way those who exercise political authority are doing their jobs, we need to ask ourselves whether the One Who put us in spiritual authority is pleased with the way we are doing our job.

I wonder how many of us have prayed for our mayor, our governor, or our president within the past month. Before we complain about the politicians and accuse them of being dishonest, we must first ask ourselves if we have been totally honest in fulfilling our responsibility.

As Christians, it is our duty to pray for all of those in authority, and that includes spiritual authority. How often do we pray for our pastor and other spiritual leaders at home and throughout the Kingdom of God?

Dr. Charles Stanley serves as pastor of the First Baptist Church in Atlanta, Georgia, which has a membership of twenty thousand. Dr. Stanley has noted that he will never enter his pulpit without knowing that his intercessors are in the prayer room praying for him. Every Sunday hundreds of people are engaged in intercessory prayer for their pastor.

Bishop Carlton Pearson is pastor of Higher Dimensions in Tulsa, Oklahoma. Scattered throughout his congregation at every service in which he preaches are intercessors, people who are stationed there for one purpose – to pray for their spiritual leader.

In Seoul, Korea, where I spent some time during my military era, there is a place called Prayer Mountain. Three hundred sixty-five days a year someone is there praying.

All these people recognize the power of intercessory prayer. So should we. But we must also understand that intercession is not judgment.

INTERCESSION IS NOT JUDGMENT

Who art thou that judgest another man's servant? to his own master he standeth or falleth.

Romans 14: 4

Some time ago a dear brother in the faith who had greatly influenced my ministry went through a very difficult, trying time in his life. When we see a brother overtaken in a fault the one thing we should learn from it is that we are never to put our faith in man – but in God. As Christians, it is not our job to judge the men and women of God, but to intercede for them.

After this brother had been interviewed about the situation, his wife was asked some questions. Both of them were in tears as she said, "I want you all to understand that I am not crying because of what my husband did. I am crying because of what has been said about him. I am crying because perhaps I was not praying for him the way I should have been."

Many Christians thought the situation was a big joke, just something to make fun about and laugh at. But many of those same people never uttered the name of that man of God in prayer.

In his writings, the Apostle Paul tells us that it is not our job to judge God's servants, but to pray for them, to make intercession for them.

Intercessory prayer is not just for those who feel a special calling to intercede. Intercession is the duty and responsibility of every believer. As Christians, each one of us is to "make up the hedge" and "stand in the gap" for others - for all men, for those in authority, and for those in our lives who cannot or do not know how to pray for themselves.

We may have a family member who is involved in things we know are not pleasing to God, things that are immoral or even illegal. Because we are in right relationship with the Lord, it is our job to pray for that person, interceding on his or her behalf with the Father. God has promised that if we do that, He will honor our prayer.

If we will intercede, God will intervene.

If you and I will stop judging and start interceding, it will affect not only our own lives, but also the lives of all those for whom we are praying.

Intercessory prayer is not just for those involved in the Charismatic Movement. It is for every believer regardless of denominational affiliation. Whether we are Baptists or Catholics or members of the Church of God in Christ, we are to be intercessors.

Every church in the Body of Christ needs to have some mode of intercessory prayer. Why? Because intercession is powerful. It produces results, as we see in Acts 12 which contains one of the greatest accounts of intercessory prayer ever recorded.

PRAYER FOR PETER

Now about that time Herod the king stretched forth his hands to vex certain of the church.

And he killed James the brother of John with the sword.

And because he saw it pleased the Jews, he proceeded further to take Peter also. (Then were the days of unleavened bread).

And when he had apprehended him, he put him in prison, and delivered him to four quaternions of soldiers to keep him; intending after Easter to bring him forth to the people.

Peter therefore was kept in prison: but prayer was made without ceasing of the church unto God for him.

Acts 12; 1-5

Peter was preaching the Word of God with power and many people were saved. But King Herod began to persecute the church in Jerusalem. He had James executed, and when he saw that it pleased the devout Jews, he had Peter arrested and thrown in prison awaiting trial.

129

While Peter was in jail, a group of the members of the church met to offer up special prayer for him. So the church in Jerusalem was *interceding* for Peter. Notice what happened as a result of their earnest intercession.

PETER'S RELEASE

And when Herod would have brought him forth, the same night Peter was sleeping between two soldier, bound with two chains: and the keepers before the door kept the prison.

And, behold, the angel of the Lord came upon him, and a light shined in the prison: and he smote Peter on the side, and raised him up, saying, Arise up quickly. And his chains fell off from his hands.

And the angel said unto him, Gird thyself, and bind on the sandals. And so he did. And he saith unto him, Cast thy garment about thee, and follow me.

And he went out, and followed him; and wist not that it was true which was done by the angel; but thought he saw a vision.

When they were past the first and second ward, they came unto the iron gate that leadeth unto the city;

which opened to them of his own accord: and they went out, and passed on through one street; and forthwith the angel departed from him.

And when Peter was come to himself, he said, Now I know of a surety, that the Lord hath sent his angel, and hath delivered me out of the hand of Herod, and from all expectation of the people of the Jews.

Acts 12:6-11

While Peter was asleep between two guards, God dispatched an angel to the prison where he was being carefully guarded. In the middle of the night, the angel tapped Peter on the side and told him to get up and get dressed. Peter's chain fell off of him, and the angel guided him out through the iron gates of the prison into the street where the angel disappeared, leaving Peter to find his way from there. Peter then realized that what had happened to him was not a vision or a dream, but was real.

Why did this event take place? Why did God send His angel to deliver Peter from the hand of Herod and the Jewish people who wanted him dead? Because the church was praying and interceding on Peter's behalf.

The Church Prayed, But Did Not Believe

And when he had considered the thing, he came to the house of Mary the mother of John, whose surname was Mark; where many were gathered together praying.

And as Peter knocked at the door of the gate, a damsel came to hearken, named Rhoda.

And when she knew that it was Peter's voice, she opened not the gate for gladness, but ran in, and told how Peter stood before the gate.

And they said unto her, Thou art mad. But she constantly affirmed that it was even so. Then said they, It is an angel.

But Peter continued knocking: and when they had opened the door, and saw him, they were astonished.

But he, beckoning unto them with the hand to hold their peace, declared unto them how the Lord had brought him out of the prison...

Acts 12:12-17

After he had thought about the situation for a while, Peter decided to go to Mary's house where the church was gathered together praying for him. When he got there and knocked on the door, a young girl came to answer it. Recognizing his voice, she ran back and told the others that Peter was at the door. But they were all so spiritual they did not believe it was really him. They thought it was an angel. When the girl insisted it was Peter, they even accused her of being crazy. The question is why offer prayer for something without believing God will answer that prayer? Let me give you an example from everyday life. Suppose we need a job, so we pray and ask God to provide us one. Then when we get that job, we immediately run to our best friend and say, "I can't believe I got the job!"

If we can't believe, then why do we waste our time praying? I don't know about you, but when I pray about something, I expect God to answer. I have an attitude of prayer.

AN ATTITUDE OF PRAYER

Pray without ceasing.

1 Thessalonians 5:17

What we must remember is that prayer – especially intercessory prayer – is a form of spiritual warfare. Every time we set ourselves to pray in agreement, we bring God on the scene. That's why Paul exhorted us to pray for all men with all kinds of prayers, intercessions, and thanksgiving. He knew that intercessory prayer is powerful.

Paul also told us to pray always, to pray without ceasing. As we have seen, we need to be continually in prayer. Our daily lives need to be marked by an attitude of prayer.

I belong to an intercessory group of pastors. When we wake up in the morning, the first thing we do is get on the telephone to one another and begin interceding. That is a wonderful way to start the day.

When you wake up in the morning, before you get your first cup of coffee, talk to the Lord. You will be amazed at how better your day will go. When you develop an attitude of prayer, it will be difficult for you to be defeated.

Even if you fail to pray for yourself, you can be secure knowing that someone else is praying for you, just as you are praying for someone else who may have failed to pray for himself or herself. That's why all of us need to become intercessors for each other.

Before many of my services, I go into the sanctuary of the church and pray for those who will be attending. Often I stop at each seat and pray for the person who will be sitting in that place. Many times people are moved to come to the Lord or to discern and obey the will of God because someone has been in earnest, heartfelt prayer for them.

As a pastor, part of my duty is to pray and intercede for those in my care. But my prayer responsibility doesn't stop there. Likewise, as Christians part of our duty is to pray and intercede for one another. But our prayer responsibility doesn't stop there either. As followers of

Christ and His example, we are also to pray for others –
even those who oppose us and persecute us.

JESUS' INTERCESSION FOR TRANSGRESSORS

**Therefore will I divide him a portion with the great,
and he shall divide the spoil with the strong; because he
hath poured out his soul unto death: and he was
numbered with the transgressors; and he bare the sin of
many, and made intercession for the transgressors.**

Isaiah 53:12

In Isaiah 53:4-12, the prophet spoke of the sacrifice
of God's own Son Jesus for the redemption of all mankind.
In verse 12 Isaiah ends the description of Jesus' sufferings
with the statement that He bore the sin of us all and made
intercession for the transgressors, meaning that He prayed
for the very ones who crucified Him, saying... **Father,
forgive them; for they know not what they do... (Luke
23:34).**

Just as Jesus interceded for His crucifiers then, so
He interceded for us today, because when we sin against
God, it breaks His heart just as it broke His heart when evil
men rejected and crucified His Son in the Bible days.

In Matthew 4:43-45 Jesus told His disciples: **Ye
have heard that it hath been said, Thou shalt love thy
neighbour, and hate thine enemy. But I say unto you,**

Love your enemies, bless them that curse you, do good to them that hate you, and pray for them which despitefully use you, and persecute you; that ye may be the children of your Father which is in heaven: for he maketh his sun to rise on the evil and on the good, and sendeth rain on the just and on the unjust.

If Jesus could intercede on the cross for those who ridiculed Him, spat on Him, placed a crown of thorns on His head, flogged Him, nailed His hands and feet to a cross, and would later stick a spear into His side, then surely you and I can pray in our comfortable homes and churches for those who criticize us and do us wrong.

For example, if one of our co-workers on the job dislikes us and tries to cause trouble for us out of spite, instead of getting angry at that person and reacting hatefully, we should adopt the attitude that Jesus displayed. We should pray for that individual, asking God to forgive him or her for the harm that has been done to us.

God has said that there is a reward for those who sacrifice themselves for the sake of others, and that is what we do when we intercede for others – especially our enemies. Whether we realize it or not, prayer does work, because it brings God on the scene,

WE PRAY, GOD ACTS

If my people who are called by my name, shall humble themselves, and pray, and seek my face and

turn from their wicked ways; then will I hear from heaven, and will forgive their sin, and will heal their land. -2 Chronicles 7:14

There will not be a healing in this land until the people of God begin to do what they are supposed to do, and that is pray. If we want to see our nation healed and restored, we must go before God praying for those in authority, for our neighbors, for our families, for our fellow believers, for ourselves, and even for our enemies. Because God has promised that if we pray, He will act.

For the believer, every problem is a prayer problem because there is no problem that cannot be solved by prayer.

Prayer works. Prayer changes things. It also changes people. That's why we don't have to worry about problems with other people, because we have the power of prayer on our side. In my own life, I don't have an enemy in the world. I can honestly say that there is no one on earth I do not like.

Now there may be people who don't like me. There may be people who think of me as their enemy. But even if they do, I don't think of them that way. One reason I don't hold grudges against other people is that I know it interferes with answered prayer. Like the psalmist, **I know that if I regard iniquity in my heart, the Lord will not**

hear me (Psalm 66:18). But I also know that if God does hear me, I have the petitions I desire of Him (1 John 5:15).

Is it really worth being mad at someone else or holding a grudge against someone else if it costs us the answers to our prayers? If it's not worth it, then wouldn't it be wise to forgive that individual so that God will hear and respond to our prayers? Isn't it worth it to forgive and bless our enemies, so God can forgive us and bless us?

Prayer does work, but it only works for those who forgive, those who overcome evil with good.

OVERCOME EVIL WITH GOOD

Be not overcome of evil, but overcome evil with good.

Romans 12:21

If I learn that anyone thinks of me as his enemy, I do my best to bless his socks off! I have been told that there are some people in New Orleans who don't really care for me, especially because of what God is doing for us at Beacon Light Baptist Church. I can't wait to run across one of those people. If I can find one of them in a restaurant, I will buy their lunch. Why would I do such a thing? Because I know that is the way to overcome evil – by doing good.

Whenever I meet someone I know doesn't like me or who has a grudge against me, I am not content to shake hands with him. I insist on giving that person a hug.

That's the way to deal with enemies. It is just such people as that we ought to be praying for.

I believe that is one reason God is blessing us so much at our church, because we know how to treat our enemies. But we also know that when God begins to bless, the devil begins to mess.

GOD BLESSES, SATAN MESSES!

The thief cometh not, but for to steal, and to kill and to destroy: I am come that they might have life, and that they might have it more abundantly.

John 10:10

Jesus said that He came to this earth to bring life in all its abundance. But He also said that the enemy comes only to steal, kill, and destroy. That is true. Any time God begins to bless, the devil begins to mess.

Every time we make up our mind to do the will of God, we can expect three things: 1) pain, 2) difficulty and 3) opposition. The devil sends those things on God's people to try to discourage us from doing what is right. That's why when we decide to study God's Word and pray, we must trust in Him with all our heart and lean not our own understanding.

THE NEED FOR PRAYER

And judgment is turned away backward, and justice standeth afar off: for truth is fallen in the street, and equity cannot enter.

Isaiah 59:14

In this passage, the Old Testament prophet Isaiah is prophesying of the future. He is saying that there will come a time when there will be no judgment, no justice. Nobody will be fair. Nobody will do the right thing. No one will bother with being honest. Everyone will be out to get whatever they can for themselves. Truth will be fallen in the streets, and equity will not even enter into the picture.

Is that not an accurate description of the times in which you and I now live? Does that not tell us why prayer is so vitally important today when truth is falling all around us daily?

TRUTH IS FALLING

Yea, truth faileth; and he that departeth from evil maketh himself a prey. And the Lord saw it, and it displeased him that there was no judgment. - Isaiah 59:15

140

What does Isaiah mean when he says that anyone who departs from evil makes himself prey? He simply means the society in which we live today has become so corrupt that those of us who try to do right make ourselves the target of all those who laugh and scorn at righteousness.

When you and I take a stand for things like honesty and integrity, people today will make fun of us. They will make jokes about us. We will become a laughingstock to them. Why? Because truth has failed. God has seen that there is no justice in this land, and it displeases Him. That's why He is looking for intercessors.

GOD IS LOOKING FOR INTERCESSORS

And he saw that there was no man, and wondered that there was no intercessor: therefore his arm brought salvation unto him; and his righteousness, it sustained him.

For he put on righteousness as a breastplate, and an helmet of salvation upon his head; and he put on the garment of vengeance for clothing, and was clad with zeal as a cloke.

Isaiah 59:16, 17

141

God is looking for those who will "make up the hedge" and "stand in the gap" on behalf of His people. Throughout the Bible we have seen examples of men of God interceding on behalf of others. That is what each of us is called to do.

In my role as pastor, I am constantly interceding on behalf of other people. Many times I will be in what I call "fellowship prayer" when the Lord will call to my mind the faces of those in need of prayer. Sometimes it may be someone I don't even know. I will stop and say, "Lord, I recognize that person even though I don't even know her name. But, Father, You know her, and You know her need. Whatever it may be, I pray that You will meet it in the name of Jesus."

When you are in prayer and suddenly someone's name or face comes across your mind that is the Holy Spirit prompting you to intercede for that person. You may not know anything about what he or she is going through at the moment, but you can still pray for that individual. If you are in right relationship with the Lord, your prayer will have an effect upon that person's life wherever he or she may be.

Isaiah says that when God could not find an intercessor, sustained by His righteousness He took it upon Himself to bring salvation to those in need. Today the Lord wants us to be His intercessors on behalf of the land. He wants to sustain us by His righteousness and use us to bring salvation and blessings to those in need.

There are people all around us – many of whom we love dearly – who will never pray for themselves. Their lives are literally in our hands. We must learn to pray not only for ourselves, but also for all those the Lord places on our heart. As soldiers of the cross, we are called to wage spiritual warfare through powerful intercessory prayer.

CALLED TO INTERCEDE

I will therefore that men pray everywhere, lifting up holy hands.....

1Timothy 2:8

Sometimes we talk more to our spouses than we do to God. How close can we be to someone with whom we never have fellowship or communion? That's why God has called me to teach His people about the vital importance of prayer- not only ourselves but also for others.

Too often Christians act as if they are totally unaware that as children of God they are called by their Heavenly Father to a life of prayer.

If you have been wondering what God is calling you to do with your life, here is His answer:

You are called to intercede!

As a believer, your entire life is to be saturated with prayer. You are called to be a part of the great company of intercessors everywhere who daily lift up their hands in prayer on behalf of God's people. If you are ready to answer the call to intercession, begin by praying this simple prayer of commitment.

Prayer

Father, I have come to see that it is my job to intercede because I am an intercessor. I may not be able to quote a lot of Scripture or preach a sermon, but I can pray. I can come before You on behalf of others.

Lord, I commit to pray regularly for all men- for those in positions of authority, for spiritual leaders, for my pastor and church. For my family and relatives, for my friends and neighbors, for my employer and co-workers, and for all those in need whom You bring to my mind and lay on my heart. Thank You, Father, for this privilege of serving You by lifting up holy hands in prayer in the name of Jesus, A-men.

ENDNOTES

Chapter 1
[1]James Strong, "Hebrew and Chaldee Dictionary," in *Strong's Exhaustive Concordance of the Bible* (Nashville: Abingdon, 1980), p.32, entry #1996, s.v. "Lucifer," Isaiah 14:12.

Chapter 3
[2]James Strong, "Greek Dictionary of the New Testament," in *Strong's Exhaustive Concordance of the Bible* (Nashville: Abingdon, 1980), p.57, entry #4074, s.v. "Peter," Matthew 16:18.

Chapter 4
[3] Strong, "Greek," p.16, entry #746, s.v. "principalities," Ephesians 6:12.
[4] Strong, "Greek," p.16, entry #746, s.v. "principalities," Ephesians 6:12.
[5] Strong, "Greek," p.43, entry #2888, s.v. "rulers," Ephesians 6:12.

BIOGRAPHY OF
BISHOP DARRYL SYLVESTER BRISTER

Bishop Darryl Sylvester Brister is the Second Presiding Bishop in the Full Gospel Baptist Church Fellowship International and was born in New Orleans, Louisiana on September 26, 1966. He received his license to preach in 1989 and was ordained on May 1, 1992, under the administration of Bishop Paul S. Morton, Sr. On January 26, 1996, at the age of 29; he was consecrated to the highest position in the church, the office of a "Bishop." He is the Apostle/Overseer of Beacon Light International Ministries and Senior Pastor and Teacher of Beacon Light International Baptist Cathedral New Orleans since 1993, where the membership exceeded 7,000 active members before Hurricane Katrina.

Bishop Darryl S. Brister

During Hurricane Katrina, all of the church buildings in New Orleans were completely destroyed and all of the members of the Beacon Light Family were dispersed across the United States. Bishop Brister has served tirelessly since the storm and has worked to rebuild the Cathedral, which will reopen during the Summer of 2014. Beacon Light International Baptist Cathedral in New Orleans is once again a thriving ministry in the city of New Orleans that continues rebuilding one day at a time.

Bishop Brister has ministered the Word of God in several countries such as Japan, Holland, Panama, Korea, Iceland, Africa, Trinidad, Tortola, and Europe. Bishop Brister attended Louisiana State University and later joined and received honorable discharge from the United States Army. He received a Bachelor of Theology Degree from McKinley Theological Seminary, a Master of Arts in Biblical Studies, a Doctor of Ministry and a Doctor of Philosophy in Religious Studies from Friends International Christian University.

Understanding that ministry exceeds beyond the confines of the church, Bishop Brister is a man on a mission to reach lost souls. As President & CEO of DSB International Ministries, a non-profit organization, Bishop Brister, reaches those incarcerated by providing them with spiritual reading materials and daily devotionals. The Darryl S. Brister Scholarship Fund supports graduating seniors entering into college and assists high school students with the purchase of school uniforms.

Bishop Brister has received numerous awards and his leadership ability has been recognized throughout the world. In April 2010, he was inducted into the Morehouse College Martin Luther King Jr. Board of Preachers. He was featured in the 1995 November edition of Ebony Magazine as one of the "Top 50 Leaders of Tomorrow," the January 2000 issue of Upscale Magazine's "Millennium Tribute to America's Most Outstanding Pastors," the September/October 2002 & 2005 issue of Gospel Today as one of "The World's Most Loved Pastors," and the 2004 New Orleans City Business Success Guide. Most recently, Bishop Brister has been featured in the Who's Who of Houston, TX and was featured on the cover of an edition of Epitome Magazine in 2013.

Bishop Brister has authored nine books that have ministered to thousands entitled, *Exposing the Enemy, The Monster Within, Recovering From Ruptured Relationships, Don't Fight the Process, Talk To Me Afterwards, Look To the Hills, Living the Dream, Doing Right In A Wrong World* and most recently *Against All Odds: Turning Obstacles into Opportunities.* In March of 1999, Bishop Brister and the Beacon Light Mass Choir released their first CD entitled, *It's All About Him.*

He serves as President and Founder of the Darryl S. Brister Bible College and Theological Seminary, which was established in August 1999 and is the Founder of the Beacon Light Christian Academy, which was established in August 2002. He is the Apostle/Overseer of the Beacon Light Baptist Church of Houma, LA, Beacon Light Baptist Church of Hammond, LA, Beacon Light Baptist Church of Baton Rouge, LA, Beacon Light of Haiti at New Orleans, and Beacon Light Community Church of Panama City, FL. Bishop Brister birthed Beacon Light International Cathedral of Houston, TX after Hurricane Katrina, which is currently in an inactive status.

Bishop Darryl S. Brister is married to Dionne Flot Brister and is the father of five children. He is a man of vision whose life embraces destiny and purpose. He has a deep hunger to win souls for Christ and is committed to serving God, is dedicated to following wherever God may lead, and excited as God continues to do "A Brand New Thing" within his life and ministry.

FOREWORD BY PAUL S. MORTON SR.

EXPOSING THE ENEMY

DARRYL S. BRISTER